CRYSTALS

Crystal Healing for Beginners Discover the Healing
Power of Crystals and Healing Stones to Heal the
Human Energy

(Unearthing the Power of Gemstones for Positive
Life Change)

Robert Jeffrey

Published By Jackson Denver

Robert Jeffrey

Crystals: Crystal Healing for Beginners Discover the Healing Power of Crystals and Healing Stones to Heal the Human Energy (Unearthing the Power of Gemstones for Positive Life Change)

ISBN 978-1-77485-356-6

Legal & Disclaimer

The information contained in this book is not designed to replace or take the place of any form of medicine or professional medical advice. The information in this book has been provided for educational and entertainment purposes only.

The information contained in this book has been compiled from sources deemed reliable, and it is accurate to the best of the Author's knowledge; however, the Author cannot guarantee its accuracy and validity and cannot be held liable for any errors or omissions. Changes are periodically made to this book. You must consult your doctor or get professional medical advice before using any of the

TABLE OF CONTENTS

Introduction

Crystals have been used for a long time and played a significant role in the human world since the prehistoric era. With their stunning colors, unusual forms as well as textures they could appear to be something completely extraordinary and it's not surprising that they were utilized for magical events rituals, religious ceremonies and for initiations.

How early man was able to discover their healing properties , we'll never know, but much of knowledge about the role of crystals for healing and magic originates from the ancient times of Egypt. They might not be the first to have discovered these properties, but they were the first to write them down to be recorded for the future.

Since the year 500,000 BC which is when the first crystal tools made of clear quartz were discovered in a cave in Beijing crystals are a part of daily lives, in a way or another. While our understanding of crystals has grown , and they've become a vital element of modern-day programs however, people's fascination for their mystical and healing properties hasn't diminished. Actually, the opposite is true.

Beautiful objects, yet also powerful healing tools which have an impact on the our psyche and body are just beginning to grasp and crystals remain awe-inspiring to us. It wasn't until recently we discovered that healing occurs not just on physical levels but also on spiritual and emotional levels too.

There are also chakrubs which are sex toys made of minerals that work directly from the inside. A quartz egg is, for instance, designed to cleanse and release energy following its introduction in the vagina. Women have reported that the energy flow at first was overwhelming, and this does not mean that they are experiencing orgasm, but satisfaction but general satisfaction.

When you are using a proper crystal therapy the different stones are put on various areas that make up the human body. Moonstone is known to increase emotions and amethyst can have a soothing impact. Citrine is also known as"the stone for success,". It is the yellow-colored version of quartz. It is a luck stone and increases optimism. The green aventurine holds the power of wealth and opens new possibilities. Rose quartz, an extremely sought-after stones - is a source of positive energy when it comes to the love area, as well as when working. Managers place it on their desk to let the energy circulate through the office. Katy Perry once said that carrying a rose quartz inside her pocket, she won't be single for long.

If you're looking to experience the benefits of crystals in a more visual way and visually, think about the use of crystals as cosmetic treatment that is very popular. If you apply an illuminating rose quartz over the skin can help you look younger as the crystal improves lymphatic system, and it is a detoxifying, visible decongestant result. It is believed to give youthful skin a new lease of energy. Amethyst soothes skin and makes pimples and redness disappear. Hollywood stars such as Jennifer Aniston and Emma Stone are adamant about the beauty of crystals and are regularly handled by New York beautician Georgia Alice. If you aren't convinced by the spiritual world, you might consider the latest trends in beauty.

The beauty of crystals is the fact that they can detect the vibrations of their surroundings and, in the case of negative energy convert it into something beneficial and positive. If it is positivity, the crystals can to amplify it to the benefit of everyone who are in such a place.

The ancient wisdom and practices which we shrewdly dismissed as myths or old wives' stories is something we're currently trying to bring back to the world of. Unfortunately, a large portion of it is irreparably lost, however as ever more people attempt to deal with the ever-increasing pressure and uncertainty of our modern world, the demand for wisdom from the past is more vital than ever.

The ancient Greeks had the most important questions regarding what it takes to live a happy life. Some of their theories regarding morality and joy have now been confirmed by the latest research. Let's hope that the change in the human mind that is currently underway can help to restore the role crystals once held within human society.

How do Crystals Work

At this point, you will likely begin to understand the importance of being able to keep your chakras in balance. Although researchers are still examining connections between the spiritual, mental, emotional, and physical worlds your chakras are supported by many thousands of years of experience. Many people over the years and across the globe have discovered that taking the proper care of their chakras is a proven way to improve their physical and mental health as well as to fight off serious illnesses.

Actually most of the potential problems mentioned above that could result from chakra imbalances can be to be quite scary - you did not realize that illnesses in organs of major importance could be influenced by something similar to our energy system. However, it's not surprising because everyone is composed of energy and how our energy interacts with the energy of our environment naturally has an impact on our bodies.

Naturally, this can be beneficial however, in the majority of cases the harmful toxins and energy sources that we are exposed to can have a negative influence on us.

It's the reason crystals are crucial. Even if you try to eat healthy or decrease your carbon footprint or train often, your chakras require a stimulation to keep them in perfect balance. The healing crystals are an answer to unlocking your unlimited potential for health and wellness within your body and mind.

It's crazy, maybe for those who aren't acquainted with the idea. What is the possibility that a rock could possess any kind of healing mechanisms? We'll explain.

As we have mentioned the primary aspect of maintaining your chakras in balance is that their vibrational frequencies are operating at optimal levels. A disturbance can result due to a problem, which can cause the pattern of vibration to shift. In the end, we are feeling out of balance whether in our mental or physical capacity or both. Healing crystals are able to control these patterns and bring harmony in our chakras.

Simply put crystals, just like other things in our world possess their own unique resonance patterns. However, healing crystals produce some of the purest frequencies due to their natural and balanced structure. The frequencies they provide our chakras function as tuning forks and bring an energy field to the frequency where it resonates optimally, and thereby creating harmony and health. However, you have to let yourself be physically, mentally and spiritually open to these changes and this is a challenge for non-believers.

If you're one of those who doubts the benefits of healing crystals, it's crucial to be aware that there is actually an aspect of science to the practice. Imagine this in this manner It's a fact that, despite the distinctions of liquids, gasses and solids, nothing can ever be truly "solid;" rather, all solid substances are comprised of a number of atoms moving as well as minerals and molecules. So, the atoms which move around us possess the energy of.

Human beings, then, are complex creatures, comprised of energy fields which embody the balance of nature and its organizational qualities. As the chakra patterns we have are different and unique, so are the crystals. The way in the frequency of each crystal resonates best to certain chakras. To heal our whole being and holistically, we should select certain crystals that are most compatible with the chakras of our society that might have been affected by an imbalance. Each crystal is a participant in nature, and has a significant reason for being there.

Chapter 1: The Historical Utilization

Of Crystals

The use of crystals for healing purposes is not a new age idea. It is an idea that has been used for centuries. Let's take a look at some fascinating facts regarding the past and its connection on crystals and healing.

Crystals' use to aid in the process of healing could be traced to the 1500 B.C as evidenced by documents from the Ebers papyrus found in Egypt. This document is a medical texts and there are references to healing with crystals in the.

* The ancient Egyptians also believed in not only the healing, but also the protection powers of crystals. It is evident from the behavior of pharaohs who wore crystals on their hairdressers and also carried amulets made of crystals. Similar objects have been found in tombs of the Egyptians. There was a widespread belief

that crystals could help the rulers become more effective, which is why they embellished their masks, as well as other accessories with crystals. Numerous items made of two crystals that are popular Amazonite and lapis were discovered inside the burial chamber of the King Tut. A gold-plated mask worn by King Tut is believed to have Amazonite inside it.

* Crystals also have a position in Chinese medicine. They were utilized to aid in the process of healing. This practice goes back up to 500 years ago. In both pranic healing as well as healing through the Chinese practices of Acupuncture crystal needles are commonly used.

* Tibetan Buddhists and the Ayurvedic method that heals have each acknowledged the importance of crystals , and have used crystals for centuries. For both Hinduism and Buddhism crystals are extremely well-known.

* The sacred scriptures from the past of India that are related to Hinduism are referred to as Vedas and they are more than five thousand years old. The Vedas go over in great detail the many properties and uses of crystals as well as how they can be utilized to heal. There are certain crystals that are recommended to treat specific ailments that are mentioned in the Vedas as well as a thorough explanation of the different power as well as the properties and properties of different crystals. For instance, it's stated within the Vedas that emeralds can bring prosperity and happiness.

* There are references to crystals multiple times in the Bible. For instance within the Old Testament, it was mandatory for the high priests that they dress in "holy clothes" which were focused around their breastplates. Moses was instructed by God to design the breastplates of high priests by using 12 crystals which had to be included in the structure.

The New Testament, New Jerusalem is thought as God's Heavenly city, is believed by many to have been built on base of the crystals. The passage in the New Testament supporting this belief mentions that the wall that was constructed within the walls of New Jerusalem was constructed out of Jasper and it was constructed from pure gold. The walls' foundations were made of various precious stones. The first layer, which is the foundation, was composed comprised of Jasper and the second was sapphire; the third comprised of Chalcedony and the fourth layer was made of Emerald and the fifth was Sardonyx and the sixth Sardius The seventh was Chrysolite and the eighth beryl and topaz comprised the ninth layer. The 10th layer is Chrysoprasus and the eleventh an emerald; and the 12th was amethyst.

* Two medical treatises written in 1150 and 1150 respectively by the saint Hildegard mention crystals. She

documented the healing properties of various crystals as well as their many applications. A description of the energy produced by crystals and the ways in which this energy assisted in healing ailments and giving strength to weak people are outlined in these reports. Saint Hildegrad was known as a nun, was renowned for her achievements and throughout her life she wrote a variety of books and poems relating to medical and theology. She also made music, and served as a doctor and scientist orator, preacher, and even a counselor to popes and kings. Her achievements make her an extraordinary woman today and even more so if she was alive in the 1100's.

* Even within the Muslim culture, the usage of crystals is extremely popular. Muhammad is an important Muslim prophet is believed to wear the carnelian ring. Many consider that wearing an ring out of carnelian guarantees the fulfillment of his wishes by Allah and make the

carnelian ring extremely popular with Muslims. According to the Bible regarding Islam it is believed that Ali was a wearer of four rings, each composed from a different crystal, on his wrist. The stones included opal, turquoise, hadid thin and carnelian. Opal symbolizes dignity and grace and turquoise as it can aid in achieving victory and strength, hadid because of its strength and carnelian because of its ability to protect. Muslims are also taught to carry around their bodies a variety of stones to give them the strength, courage and endurance. They also have faith. According to some sources, the Prophet himself recommended that people wear the above mentioned stones while praying. Not only those stones but all stones are believed to possess healing properties.

* The crystal use has been widely practiced by diverse tribes throughout the globe. It was believed that the Mayans considered that the power possessed through crystals could be utilized for

healing not just both physical, mental and emotional levels but also on a spiritual level. They also used crystals for diagnosing illnesses.

* A different ancient civilization which made use of crystals to heal is the Incas. They held emerald in particular reverence and believed it to be a powerful and sacred stone. The Incas prefer to be buried in an early grave than reveal the exact location of the mines for emerald to their conquerors.

* However, in many Native American and Australian tribes crystals were used of not only to diagnose illnesses but also to treat patients.

* Even as late as the 17th century the stones were valued not just because they were expensive, but also for their magical powers. They were coveted not only by the uninitiated peasants, but the more educated too.

* Tibetan monks were believed to view quartz crystals as holy objects with great power.

* The Taoists considered quartz as an "gem of wisdom."

* In Japan Quartz crystals were thought to be an important part of the dragon's heart. In Japanese tradition, the dragons are of great significance as it symbolizes the power of wisdom and power.

* Cleopatra's preferred jewel was believed that it was a band made of Amethyst that was engraved with a representation that represented her Persian Sun God, Mithras. In addition, she was able to charmed two powerful males of Rome, Julius Caesar and Mark Anthony, it was an accepted belief among Roman females that wearing an amethyst ring would aid in ensuring they had husbands who were loyal and loyal to them.

* The saint of. Valentine is believed that He wore rings made up of amethyst ring with a portrait of cupid.

There is a belief it was Alexander the Great was believed to have worn an enormous emerald in order to in his victory in battles.

The Moghuls of India such as Shah Jahan, used to use Emeralds and inscribe Holy Scriptures on them and use the stones as talismans.

The belief is that early Sumerians believed that lapis lazuli was as a sacred stone. There is a very popular expression among Sumerian Priests, which says that anyone who wears an amulet of lapis during a battle are guaranteed to be victorious.

Chapter 2: Fundamentals of Healing

with Crystals

We are now to the fifth stage of getting success in crystal healing. This is where it is essential to master the fundamental procedures to accomplish it. Crystal healing requires the presence of mind and speech, therefore you need to be able to perform these tasks and be prepared prior to when you start the procedure.

The first thing we should master in conducting in crystal healing is to understand chakra. The term"chakra" is the Sanskrit word for wheel. Chakra generally refers to the energy wheel within our bodies which spins and turns for indefinitely as we continue to exist as living entities. Chakras cannot be seen with the naked eye, however some talented people, known as psychics, are able to see them. Many psychics visualize chakras as bright wheels or flowers with a central. The chakra of a person stretches starting from the bottom of their spinal cord to the highest point of their head. It's located on both the front and back of a body.

There are seven chakras that correspond to different areas of the body. The chakras are rotated at different speeds. The chakra that is slowest to rotate is called the primary chakra, or the one that is known as the chakra of root. While the chakra that is fastest to rotate is known as the seventh chakra often referred to as the crown chakra.

Before we begin the procedure, we should be able locate the chakras within our bodies in the first place. The first chakra, also known as the root chakra is situated at the bottom of the spine, close to the tail bone on the back, and also the pubic bone to the front. It is the place of the survival of a person security, safety, and other basic needs.

The second chakra, or the belly chakra, or sacral chakra is located on the spine . It's located just two inches beneath the navel. It is the centre of an individual's sexuality, intuition and self-worth, as well as creativity.

Third chakra often referred to as the solar plexus , is located in the center of the stomach, a couple of inches from breasts. It is the home of the ego as well as the source of an individual's anger strength, personal power, strength and desires.

The fourth chakra, or heart chakra is where love, spirituality and compassion dwell. It is situated in the center where the shoulder blades meet in the back, as well as behind the breastbone in the front.

The fifth chakra, or throat chakra acts as the one responsible that is responsible for sound, communication, and the expression of ideas and thoughts. It is located in the area that looks like an X in the clavicles in the lower neck.

The sixth chakra, also known as the one that is often referred to as the Third Eye is the chakra that is responsible for greater intuition and psychic ability and the energy that surround the light and spirit. It also aids to eliminate self-centeredness and purifying negative thoughts. It is placed on the in the upper part of the eye in the middle of your forehead.

The seventh chakra, which is the last one, is also known as"the crown chakra. It is the source of spirituality, powerful thoughts as well as cosmic consciousness, energy as well as wisdom and awakening. It is located top of the skull.

After we've discovered the different chakras and the functions they play for, let's explore the process of crystal healing.

The process of crystal healing is accomplished by placing the crystals at specific places where you believe that your chakras may be affected. If, for instance, you're experiencing problems with your digestion then you need to place a particular crystal in the area that is the stomach chakra, or second chakra. This is the reason it is essential to know the exact location of the chakras as well as the kind of crystals they are associated with so that you can determine where to place the appropriate type of crystal to ease the symptoms of ailments.

In essence, there are five steps that are essential to the process of crystal healing. The first step is to determine the type of illness the person is suffering from. The next step is to pick a stone that can most effectively heal the individual and his or his or her illness, based what the doctor has determined. A third stage is to cleanse the crystal. In the fourth, you must to be connected and attuned to the crystal you selected. The last, but certainly not the final step is to activate the crystal, program it and charge it. crystal.

What is the reason to purify your crystal? It is true that sometimes a stone is unable to connect with yourself and the chakras. The crystal you used to be familiar with may not be as pleasant in the same way it is now. If you decide to purchase the right crystal, it is impossible to know what kind of energy may be within the crystal. Crystals can accumulate of negative energy, which could cause harm to you rather than beneficial. This is the reason you should to clean your crystals prior to the time you begin using them so that they will be clean and ready for use. There are a variety of ways on how to cleanse your crystal. The easiest method is to cleansing the crystals with detergent. The best way to do this is wash the crystals with the detergent, and after that it, you should immerse them in water until soap bubbles are gone. You could also run the crystals through the faucet and let the water flow eliminate the soap, instead of submerging them. After the crystals are cleaned they can be dried off with a soft cloth or tablecloth.

Another method of purifying your crystal is by smudging that is the act using the smoke of the burned cedar or sage to the surface of the crystal. Also, there is a unique method for cleansing crystal , which is performed by using the moonlight method. This is the practice of exposing crystals to the bright light that comes from the moon's full light, and let the gentle rays from the night's glow cleanse the crystals.

After you have removed the crystal from its dirt the next step you must take is program the crystal. The process for programming crystals fairly simple. The only thing you need to do is gather every positive energy you have as well as the positive energy you get in the universe around you. then channel this energy to the crystal. It is basically the same as transferring the energy you possess within your body into your crystal to ensure that it is only positive. There are a variety of ways for programming your crystals. Many do this by placing the crystal in their palms for a few minutes. Some healers also use chants mantras, and incantations to channel the energy into the crystal. They also combine a few of these techniques. They place the crystals into their fists that are closed and make an incantation or sing an chant while they shut their eyes. They direct their energy towards the sky and allow it to flow into the crystal.

We are already familiar with the easy method of healing that involves making use of the crystal. Another question to ask is what are the conditions which it is able to treat? The next chapter will talk on this.

Chapter 3: The Way to Begin A

Crystal Collection

The Choice of a Crystal to Buy

Be sure to be knowledgeable about the crystals you acquire. The best way to pick the right crystal is to feel the energy of it. Be guided by your intuition and feeling of what is best to you. Allow yourself to be guided by the crystal, then let it guide you.

There are a variety of experiences that shoppers have to endure when selecting the right crystal. In most cases, I experience an overall good vibe as well as some tingling.

The heat emitted from stone

A speck of light emanating from the crystal

*Cold energy

*Lightheaded sensation

*Ringing Ears

*An unexpected rush of excitement

It is also important to take note of crystals you do not like. They usually are a sign of qualities or problems you must address.

Select By Crystal System

Each crystal is a part of a distinct crystal system, with distinct characteristics. The crystal systems consist of:

Hexagonal crystals that manifest

Isometric crystals can improve the quality of life and boost energy

Monoclinic crystals that protect and secure

Orthorhombic crystals that clean, purify, deblock and let go

Tetragonal crystals, that absorb or repel energy sources

Amorphous "crystals," which have distinct properties.

Colors to Choose From

The significance of color goes well beyond personal taste. Each color has its own specific vibrational energies and associated health benefits. When you select a crystal from the crystal system with the characteristics you want to exhibit and the healing characteristics that the colour embodies, you are able to choose crystals specifically to treat specific ailments.

Decide based on how they make You Feel

When choosing crystals, take it in your hands and observe how you feel. Be aware of whether or not they make you feel at ease or uncomfortable if they seem weighty or light, and when you feel any other sensations. You should experience the sensation of being comfortable.

Pairing Crystals

Similar to cheese and wine Certain crystals work well , making them more than their components. Crystals that work well together are energized in a way that actually help to focus the energy. For instance each crystal's energy can be amplified when it is paired with crystals that are clear. Here are different pairings that are successful:

Smoky Quartz along with Apache Tears - a powerful combination for people grieving.

Amethyst and Labradorite are both able to assist you to have more restful sleep.

Citrine along with Black Tourmaline - can help to ground you for prosperity.

Rose Quartz and Ruby or Garnet are great for pairing relationships

Black Tourmaline and Clear Quartz can help to facilitate the flow of unbalanced energy.

Pick using a Dowsing Rod

The idea is that it's a method that is more advanced, however novices can easily learn to use one to identify the most effective stones to start their exercise. Remember that pendulum dowsing may require more discernment.

Being one of the oldest methods of divination, pendulum-dowsing allows us to understand the power of crystals and help us to the one that is the closest to our soul. Naturally, in the process of locating the pendulum, it's essential to choose the one that is right for you to ensure a smooth and efficient experience.

When choosing a pendulum to use examine a variety of them. Your intuition will decide which is ideal for you and guide you to the best one without you having to make any effort to think. Once you've got a pendulum, you are able to begin using it to select crystals, or ask questions, or use it to help you make decisions that will result in the answer "yes or no.

The steps to using pendulum dowsers to make crystal choice:

Clear your mind prior to embarking on any procedure using crystals, make sure that your mind is free of any distractions. Spend a few minutes to pay attention to your breathing and then set your focus on the objective of the dowsing.

Practice Your Pendulum

Different pendulums resonate with different levels of intensity and quality. What feels like"yes" to one pendulum could be completely different with the other. To tune into your particular pendulum, place it in your hands then close your eyes. Ask it a question for which you're sure that the answer is yes. Once you've experienced the vibrations of a positive answer, try asking an inquiry whose answer will be non. You should be able to feel a shift in the frequency the pendulum. As you do this, you will develop an understanding of your pendulum's vibration, making it easier to be aware of where it is trying to direct you.

Select your crystals - If you are using a pendulum dowser select the crystals you want, simply place the pendulum in front of the crystal or an image depicting the crystal, if you're purchasing it from an online store and ask it questions about the crystal. Do not make any suggestions to influence the answers of the pendulum, as it may interfere with its actual recommendation. Make sure to keep your eyes open.

Where to Buy

There are numerous places that sell stones , both in brick-and-mortar shops and on the internet. Cities and towns are home to retail crystal stores. They could be referred to as crystal stores, bookshops that are metaphysical and New Age shops. They have knowledgeable personnel, the majority allow you to handle the crystals prior to purchasing. There are also gemstone or mineral shows that travel. They are an excellent place to buy crystals. They can't be beat for variety or prices.

They do require to be scheduled ahead of time. It is possible to purchase crystals online , but when making an order, make sure you're dealing with a reputable seller. It is possible to use your pendulum to purchase crystals on the internet.

Crystal Starter Kit

Clear Quartz - If you aren't sure which crystal to select, you can start with clear quartz. It can work with any kind of energy.

Smoky Quartz is the stone most people prefer as it's an amplification stone that transforms negativity into positivity.

Citrine is a self-esteem booster and wealth

Rose Quartz - helps support all kinds of love, including romantic love that is unconditional.

Amethyst aids you to connect with the intuition and guidance of higher dimensions as well as the power of desires

Black Tourmaline - is a stone of grounding that protects and keeps negativity at bay.

Rainbow Fluorite increases the senses, encourages love and promotes clear communication.

Carnelian assists you in setting the right boundaries, be honest and be innovative.

Hematite is a stone that provides protection grounded, calming, and protective and also attracts energies you'd like to bring into your life.

Turquoise is believed to bring luck as well as prosperity as well as personal strength.

The Sacred Geometry of Stones Cut

There are crystals that have been cut into a variety of shapes, like polyhedrons and spheres. These possess different characteristics. Making use of crystals cut in these shapes will enhance the properties of the crystal as well as holy shape.

Dodecahedron The dodecahedron is connected to elements in the Ethereal realm. It can connect you to intuition as well as higher realms.

Hexahedron The hexahedron or cube, is the earth element. It's grounded and stable.

Icosahedron : The icosahedron has been connected to the element water. It links you to change and flow.

Merkaba The Merkaba is a 3D star. It has all five polyhedrons mentioned above inside, and thus brings together the best qualities of each. It also represents the power of sacred truth and the eternal wisdom.

Octahedron : The octahedron symbolizes air as an element. Air and is a symbol of kindness, compassion forgiveness, love and compassion.

The sphere has the power of completeness of wholeness, oneness, and completeness.

Tetrahedron is associated with elements of fire. the tetrahedron is a symbol of stability, balance, as well as the ability to effect the possibility of change.

Other names for Crystals

In recent times, certain retailers have assigned the crystals a brand name and in some instances identified the crystals. The reason that they are labeled is that they is sourced from a specific location on the property of the person who brands it However, the location of the crystal is not a major factor in any of the characteristics that crystals possess.

Amazon Jade Amazonite.

The name Aqua Terra Jasper is made up of onyx or resin.

*Atlantis Stone is Larimar.

Azeztulite has similar properties to clear quartz.

*Boji Stones can be found without branding in the form of Kansas Pop Rocks.

*Healerite is commonly referred to as Chrysolite.

*Isis Calcite is the brand form of white calcite.

Lemurian Light Crystals is a brand-named version made from Lemurian quartz.

*Mani Stone is a white-black jasper.

*Master Shamanite is the same as black calcite.

"Merkabite" is a type of Calcite can be described as white Calcite

*Revelation Stone is red or brown jasper.

*Sauralite Azeztuline is a quartz found in New Zealand.

*Zultanite is the mineral diaspore.

*Agape Crystals comprise seven crystals that are distinct including transparent quartz, smoke, amethyst and rusticated quarts. goethite and lepidocrocite. cacoxenite.

Crystal Safety

In general working with crystals is generally safe. But, certain crystals may contain substances (such as copper, aluminum sulfur, fluorine, asbestos, strontium) that can be harmful to humans. Therefore, avoid putting them in your bathtub or create a crystal elixir using them. It is also recommended not to clean your hands once you've completed taking them in. The crystals are:

*Aquamarine (contains aluminum)

*Black Tourmaline (contains aluminum)

*Celestite (contains strontium)

*Cinnabar (contains mercury)

*Dioptase (contains copper)

*Emerald (contains aluminum)

*Fluorite (contains fluorine)

*Garnet (contains aluminum)

*Iolite (contains aluminum)

*Jade (contains asbestos)

*Kansas pop rocks (contains aluminum)

*Labradorite (contains aluminum)

*Lapis lapis lazuli (contains Pyrite, which is a source of sulfur)

*Malachite (contains copper)

*Moldavite (contains aluminum)

*Moonstone (contains aluminum)

*Prehnite (contains aluminum)

*Ruby (contains aluminum)

*Sapphire (contains aluminum)

*Sodalite (contains aluminum)

*Spinel (contains aluminum)

*Sugilite (contains aluminum)

*Sulfur (contains poisonous)

*Tanzanite (contains aluminum)

*Tigers eye, unpolished (contains asbestos)

*Topaz (contains aluminum)

*Tourmaline (contains aluminum)

*Turquoise (contains aluminum)

*Zircon (contains zirconium)

Once you have a grasp of the basics of chakras and crystals as well as their functions and function, it is time to move further and apply this knowledge using crystal grids. In simple terms it is the process of working with crystals, which involves the creation of specific geometric forms or patterns. The patterns typically include the sacred geometry in their design.

If used correctly, grids can boost the effectiveness of the crystals further. Although it is possible to obtain good results from the use of just one crystal, when you apply grids, they can just enhance the effects and give it energy a major increase.

To design your own crystal grid, you'll first must establish the foundation or base to work from. The design you choose to use could be printed on a piece fabric or on a piece of paper. There are wooden boards with engraved designs which they can spread out for their crystals to be placed on. In certain instances you can also get an outline to help you determine precisely where to put your crystals to get the most result.

Why you need them

A crystal grid for a variety of motives. They are often used for connection with the spiritual realm, but they are also utilized to heal, provide security, find love, for achieving prosperity, and a many other.

When you work with your crystal grid system, that group of crystals working in harmony is more powerful and is combined with your sacred geometry. They draw the extra energy that can help you. They also function as solid anchors when you require them.

As you may think of, there's numerous ways to design an ideal Crystal Grid, every one having their own distinct benefits for you. There are many reasons to use grids, it is possible to divide them into four distinct types.

Crystal Energy: Due to their particular structure, crystals perform exceptionally well when utilized in specific patterns. The crystal grid allows you to draw even more of their capabilities to provide you additional support to achieve your objectives.

It is crucial to select crystals with the exact properties you're looking for. In order to achieve your goal You may need think beyond the obvious but. If, for instance you want to increase your chances of being successful, then you'd surely choose crystals that aid you in achieving this goal, however, you could also consider crystals with similar properties such as determination and confidence in yourself to help you achieve it. Together with the power of each of these elements will help to guide their energies towards the direction that is best for you.

The sacred Geometry The concept of sacred geometry is a metaphysical science that argues that certain patterns observed in nature can be fingerprints that can be used to understand our universe as well as how it works. These forms are referred to as sacred geometry and symbolize the real framework of the universe.

Each of these shapes have their particular purpose and energy. Although some crystal grids do not use sacred geometry however, when it does, it makes the whole grid much stronger than one that doesn't. If you are using sacred geometry, select your grids with care so that you can ensure the strength you receive is directed toward your ultimate goal.

The use of sacred geometry is useful in helping to send your energy through the grid to the world to allow the results to be realized. It is also possible to channel that energy to heal your damaged aura to enhance your self-esteem when it is needed. The idea is that crystals possess their own distinct capabilities that can aid you, using them in conjunction with particular chakras in grids can increase their power to an even greater extent. If you utilize the crystal grid in conjunction with the sacred geometry of your grid, you can enjoy the strongest power you can get in the metaphysical realm.

Numerology: The use of crystal grids in the ancient science of numerology is like sacred geometry. When you choose the crystals you want to connect with in accordance with their symbolism and meaning when it is correlated to the grid will be able to connect with them to help you achieve your goal and more easily connect with their energy. It not only increases the energy that emanates from them, it also can channel it to help you concentrate on a specific job.

Your Intention: Do not overlook the power and energy generated through your thoughts. If you are able to transmit this information to crystals especially when they've been carefully set up on a grid, it is when they can truly perform at their highest. Crystals can be programmed with your thoughts and your dreams. The grid will keep the crystals and broadcast them to the universe for the time you want them to.

These grids can be powerful tools for you and can be extremely efficient. However, to reap the most effective results, you must adhere to your intentions to them. Their power can be an source of energy and motivation, however you won't get rewards for things you do not want to do anything about. They are only able to connect with the reality in you and communicate this intention throughout the day for all the time you want them to for you to make the changes you desire.

Chapter 4: Barite

Barite is a crystal which can be found in a variety of forms and colours. The environment within which Barite develops, it could be formed by prismatic crystals lamellar and fibrous crystalline structures. Barite's colours range from deep greens and blues all the way to browns, reds black, yellow, and sometimes even fluorescent. Barite has been observed to form into concentric crystals with tubular shapes, resulting in an appearance like flowers. These rare barites are extremely sought-after by gemstone collectors Reiki practitioner and healing practitioners alike. Barite was revered to Native Americans as a ritual stone that had potent healing properties and has been regarded as such since. Barite's energetic field has been known to boost the brain's functions, including memory recall determination, willpower, and imagination. Barite has also been utilized to increase psychic abilities, allowing regression into the past and lucid dreams, as well as contact with the otherworldly and the higher dimensions of consciousness. Barite is often used to aid in the body's detoxification process, removing toxic build-up, as well as environmental pollutants that build up within the body. It is a healing stone. Barite is one of numerous stones that can break down energy blockages. However wearing or carrying Barite for extended periods of time, for months or even years, will help keep the balance and ensure the natural flow of energy in the body's chakra and energetic networks. This improves overall health, mood, and longevity. Barite can remove negative thinking patterns that is ideal for those who is suffering from emotional pain or addiction, stress, and so on. The energy of Barite enters the chakra via it's Third Eye Chakra an is one of the stones that can actually boost the chakra energy of the body, or "chi", and therefore is highly regarded by spiritualists and people who practice meditation as well as martial arts.

Color

Green

Blue

Red

Brown

Yellow

Black

Colorless

Birthstone

No affiliation

Zodiac

Aquarius

Energetic Frequencies

Healing

Chakras

The Third Eye

Bloodstone

The Ancients were aware of Bloodstone as Heliotrope which is a name that originates from two Greek words that refer to'sun-turning and believed to safeguard the body and mind of its wearer. Therefore, it is used for centuries as a talisman to ensure well-being and a long life. The stone is believed to increase the ability to think and also protect from illnesses such as flu and colds by energizing the whole body and may improve the overall endurance of your body. Bloodstone is a form of Jasper but it typically it is a blend of Jasper as well as Quartz that has deep green shades set with vibrant red blood-like spots , and tiny flecks. Bloodstone isn't just an ornamental stone, but it also has beneficial properties for healing, which include but aren't restricted to strengthening the immune system, as well as purifying and cleansing organs like the liver, bladder spleen, and intestines and it is said that wearing the Bloodstone talisman can bring its wearer prosperity, respect, wealth as well as fame. The Bloodstone gemstone has many applications. is unique in appearance and form and energy levels. It is believed to give the wearer the strength and determination needed to succeed and is the ideal talisman for people in mourning or going through difficult situations. The stone is connected to and the Root and the Heart Chakra and works to bring balance to the body's chakra system and aura, clearing any energetic blocks, leading to higher levels of understanding that transcend our normal nature. Bloodstones are often worn by those who want to make a mark on their lives. Bloodstone is usually worn by those who want to leave their mark by earning respect, honor respect, honor, and fame.

Color

Green/Red

Birthstone

March

Zodiac

Aries

Connections to Scorpio

Energetic Frequencies

Acceptance

Magic

Sacrifice

Healing

Chakras

The Heart Chakra

The Root Chakra

Blue John

It is only found in Derbyshire England, Blue John is a stunning combination that are deep blue white, purple reds and yellow.

The highly sought-after and attractive stone is a fluorite that from Roman times was utilized to shield wearers from the negative effects of alcohol consumption. The rare stone is a favorite among collectors , with crystals that have dark purple shades being most sought-after. Blue John's energy vibrations hold various metaphysical properties, many that are derived from the strong tranquil energy that emanates out of the stone. It aids in quieting an overly busy mind by gently breaking repetitive and destructive thinking patterns. It is also known as a catalyst for personal transformation, renewal and expansion. Wearing Blue John inspires us to discover the most exciting and interesting things. Meditation using Blue John brings truth and greater insight into our lives. Its link to our Third Eye Chakra helps to connect to higher levels of consciousness. It is also believed to aid in lucid dreams. Blue John is a powerful healing stone that activates your Crown chakra and the Solar Plexus. It is believed to aid in the healing process of infections. Blue John also promotes healthy dental and bone growth , and significantly decreasing the time to heal fractures and broken bones. It is also effective to ease pain and can be extremely soothing to nerves. Blue John is used to treat irritations and inflammations of the ears, eyes, throat and nose from Ancient Rome and is well-known that it boosts the immune system as well as the elimination processes of the human body. It is a stone which can do wonders for your mind, enhancing the clarity and focus of your thoughts by bringing in and pooling the scattered and disorganized energies , and then reorienting them in a way that is best suitable to achieve our objectives. Blue John's energy is supportive and encourages us. It assists us in overcoming insanity and faulty reasoning. It makes us realize the truth within us, which may be difficult to accept however it only makes us stronger over the long term through helping us find our the true meaning. Relaxing while applying Blue John on the throat or brows is believed to give us access to knowledge and concepts that would otherwise be impossible to access. Spiritualists commonly employ Blue John to enhance clairvoyance and other psychic abilities. It is said to even open the way to the mysterious state of "No Mind or The Void.

Color

Bands with stripes of:

Blue

Purple

White

Red

Yellow

Birthstone

January

February

Zodiac

Pisces

Energetic Frequencies

Calming

Transformative

Healing

Chakras

Third Eye Chakra Third Eye Chakra

The Crown Chakra

The Solar Plexus Chakra

Brandberg Amethyst

Brandberg Amethyst is a variant from Smoky Quartz along with Amethyst, both of which are found only in Namibia specifically in the Brandberg (or Fire) Mountain situated within the Namib Desert. It is one of the rare crystals that are that are found with Enhydros (inclusions that are pure waters) as well as other uncommon imperfections, which makes it a valuable stone for healers, spiritualists or Reiki practitioners. It is a healing stone that can affect our spiritually, emotionally as well as physically, connecting us with the energy of the universe that surrounds us and instilling unconditional love in both thinking and doing. Brandberg Amethyst combines the calming effect of Amethyst with the grounding effects of Smokey Quartz leading to an effect that helps stabilize the entire body and boosts and enhances the energy of the chakra system and the aura. Brandberg Amethyst has been described as a "master healer" and is beneficial in slowing the time to recover from injury and illness as well. It aids those suffering in chronic malnutrition, fatigue, or immune deficiencies by its capacity to revitalize the body system and restore the natural flow of energy through the body and chakra system. The energy of vibration that is released by Brandberg

Amethyst, when controlled and harnessed can be utilized to relieve the pain of dental and skeletal joints. It is believed to assist in the healing process of infections that relate to the throat and ear. Brandberg Amethyst has a forceful influence both spiritually and emotionally helping people suffering from addictions and stress. It is a stone which helps us let forget past hurts as well as feelings of guilt anger and loss, as well as regret. It also helps us to forgive us and others, bringing an enduring feeling in peace within and happiness. This stone acts in a way of establishing a cosmic anchor, bringing our energy to the earth. It can also have a balancing effect on the chakras and heals the spirit by revitalizing the body, and filling the person with feelings of satisfaction and happiness.

Color

Purple

Blue

Opaque

Smokey

Light Yellow/Red

Birthstone

February

November

December

Zodiac

Aquarius

Pisces

Energetic Frequencies

Protection

Healing

Chakras

It is the Third Eye Chakra

The Crown Chakra

Brochantite

Brochantite crystal has a profound influence on the ethereal body as well as the chakra system that is the body. It is highly prized by its curative properties as well as its ability to rebalance the meridians of the body and the chakras. It typically displays a range of bright green to grey green Brochantite can also be recognized to display shades of darkest green to black. Brochantite is that is frequently utilized in meditation, because of its strong connections to higher realms of spirituality as well as the relaxing effects it can have on people who are exposed to its tranquil energy, as well as its purifying properties that transform every space in to a secure and peaceful space to practice meditation, prayers or healing. Brochantite is widely employed to help realign and center the chakras. Also, the stone has the benefit of boosting the energy of our bodies, which brings out our highest potential it bridges between spiritual and physical realms. The high level of copper in Brochantite's mineral composition makes it an excellent healing stone, and it is also known for its ability to assist those suffering from respiratory or lung ailments. It's great for those who suffer from water retention. it balances fluids in the body and regulates and ensures healthy blood flow. It has been utilized to treat diseases affecting the prostate and pancreas. Brochantite is also a shield against environmental contaminants and other toxins that are present in drinks and food that we consume every day. Brochantite stimulates curiosity, insight and imagination, making it the perfect talisman for students of all sorts. The warm energy that emanates from Brochantite helps those who are suffering from emotional trauma as well as an anxious mind. It also helps to replace fears of guilt and anxiety with feelings of happiness and tranquility. This gorgeous green stone strongly resonates to chakras like the Heart Chakra and massively boosts the ability to perceive and even psychic abilities, particularly when it is used with other stones like Bustamite, Lolite and Rainbow Moonstone.

The legend says that a Brochantite crystal loses its shine and lustre as warning signs of deceit, imminent threat or if traitors are near.

Color

Green

Black

Birthstone

August

Zodiac

Capricorn

Energetic Frequencies

Chakras

The Heart Chakra

Carnelian

Carnelian is a stone that is found in India and South America and exists in shades of orange and red, with the dark reds being most sought-after. Carnelian is recognized to be one of the rocks that promote motivation , and has strong associations with courage physical strength, courage, and courage that aid shy and introverted to take on leadership roles as well as being engaging and engaging public speaking. The name carnelian originates from the Latin word for flesh. It was in Ancient Egypt, Carnelian was called 'the sun setting as it has an orange appearance expressing female energy energies, with the red stones being associated with masculine energies. Carnelian is an energetic stone that acts as a bridge between our personal and emotional states and guides users to higher levels of autonomy. It is a healing stone Carnelian is believed to assist the body's ability to absorb minerals and nutrients, boosts and keeps blood flow circulation, and pressure.

It also clears congestion, heals haemorrhoids and helps heal bad backs, arthritis, joint pain scars and

even improve fertility. The stone acts as stabiliser stone, which helps the user to be in the present moment, that is ideal for those who dream and worry and is an ideal talisman for people who are struggling with coordination and motivation. It also is believed to enhance appetite. Carnelian in both its primary colours has close connections between Sacral (orange shades) along with Base Chakras (red hues) which provide wearers with an increased intuition (gut intuition) emotional stability as well as an atmosphere of friendship and joy.

Color

Red/Orange

Pink

Brown

Birthstone

May

July

August

Zodiac

Aries

Taurus

Virgo

Planet

Mars

Energetic Frequencies

Creativity

Healing

Power

Chakras

The Second Chakra, also known as the Sacral Chakra

The Root or Base Chakra

Celestite

A crystal with colours of clear blue tropical waters, Celestite is a relatively modern stone that was first mentioned in the late 1800s. It is famous by its blue celestial hues, but could also appear extremely light clear, white yellow, and subtle reds. Its appearance Celestite suggests that its energy is subtle and light but the vibratory frequency of Celestite and the effects they produce are powerful and effective. A part of Celestite in the North corner of your bedroom can make it a more peaceful and uplifting space. when the energy of Celestite's water infiltrates the room, it will transform into a serene place for rest, prayer and meditation. It is believed that Celestite is able to awaken psychic abilities. It is utilized by Wiccans psychics, spiritualists, psychics and healers to boost various abilities, such as telepathy, clairvoyance, and clairvoyance. remote reviewing and Telekinesis. Celestite stimulates three of the highest chakras which are the Crown Third Eye and the

Throat Chakras providing the body with light energy giving us insight and empowering us with the honesty and increasing our fortitude so that we can be able to remain on the right route. Celestite is among the few stones connected directly with the Eighth Chakra known as the Soul Star Chakra, the only chakra located outside the body. It is connected to field of energy on earth. It is believed to play an important part in the process of spiritual awakening by its connection to spiritual beings and opening the way to divine wisdom. Celestite is a stone which enhances and complements the properties of other crystals, such as those belonging to the Quartz family. It also enhances the qualities of Moldavite along with Pollucite. Celestite is believed to enhance the mind and help balance emotions. It is also a cleanser for the aura and body, and also stimulates our body's detoxification process. It is used for treating throat, eye and ear ailments and is believed to benefit people recovering from brain or head injury. The energy released by Celestite is a wonder for chronic pain and stress Its vibrations can penetrate and relax the body relaxing muscles, regulating the heart rate and stomach function. It is a talisman. Celestite acts as a dispeller that energizes the body when it eliminates negative emotional accumulation which could block the chakras or the aura. It alleviates anxiety and guilt as well as fearful thoughts by redirecting our energy and focus to positively oriented aspects in life. This makes Celestite valuable as well as beautiful.

Color

Light Blue

White

Clear

Yellow

Red

Citrine's name comes in its French word citron which means "lemon" but is often referred to as as the Merchant's Stone due to its incredible ability to boost account balances, and also its status as the Stone of the Mind due to the belief of the past that the placing of the Citrine Stone on your forehead could bring out the person's psychic abilities. Natural Citrine is radiant and pure yellow stone, with sometimes transparent golden hues that emit powerful frequencies that neutralize the negative energies and provide a space that is conducive to only the highest and most happy of moods. It is believed that Citrine helps in the removal of bodily toxins, and aids in maintaining an ideal digestive system. It also is believed to help with the circulation of blood, blood detoxification and to maintain an ideal thyroid. Citrine is most commonly a happy stone that helps to remove doubt and inadequacy from a person's life and replace it with confidence, strength and a clear mind. It has associations that are associated with chakras like the Crown, Solar Plexus and Sacral Chakra and boasts the ability to align, balance and enhance the chakra network , which allows for greater synergy between the both mind and body that boosts the immune system, as well as the ability to be creative and enhances our intellectual and psychic abilities. Citrine is a wonderful stone to meditate on and is one of the "Seeker Stones', which can be used as a talisman that can alter lives by leading the user toward new perspectives like a compass , guiding us to new knowledge and new beginnings.

Color

A Yellow Color With Dark Brown Hues

Birthstone

November

Zodiac

Cancer

Gemini

Chapter 5: Crystal Mythology

Myths and myths played a important role in the development of human civilization they were extremely influential beliefs that people employed to explain the illogical. Although many legends and myths are difficult to comprehend or even be believed today, some proved to be true about actual events that occurred, and presented in a manner that people of the day could comprehend.

Gemstones and crystals, which are precious and exquisite have played an important role in the ancient mythology. The people who used them had the hopes of transmitting to themselves the characteristics of the stones they used, such as beauty, strength, power, etc.

A number of historians and enthusiasts has attempted to compile a collection of crystal-related myths which would encompass stories from across the globe however, it turned out to be an impossible task. Crystals had different meanings in different cultures, and as myths, were often used to explain concepts in according to the religion of the region. The tales of how specific crystals were created needed to be based on local geography and also the gods that were local to the area.

The same is true for color. Colors are symbolic of different things for different cultures, and an all-encompassing explanation of what a stone of a particular color represents isn't likely. For instance in Western society the black color is a symbol of death, and mourners wear black during funerals. In contrast in the Far East people, utilize white as a symbol of dying (India or Japan) and wear white attire at funerals.

Nowadays, as globalization grows and cultures disappear, melting into one the other, what we typically think of as a myth associated with an individual tradition is actually revealed to be a blend of different beliefs from various styles, religions, and times.

In Neolithic times, possibly even earlier, crystals were utilized as amulets and charms that provide protection, strength and wisdom. For certain semi-precious stones the "amuletic" power could be explained through the nature of their properties:

The connection of cornelian to blood, and also with Zoroastrian worship of fire.

The unique reflective qualities of crystal

The slight electrical surge and amber scent when it is rubbed

The iridescence of mother-of pearl, cat's eye, and the opal

The striking patterns of jasper and agate.

The obsidian's hardness is a testament to its durability.

The turquoise color is linked with the skies and rain , bringing the power of nature, and also its characteristic "to age"and equates it to the cycle of life

In the past, Babylonians, Greeks, Romans and Egyptians all believed in the semi-precious stones, and utilized them as talismans, medicinal makeup items, burial and other objects. As soon as crystals were incorporated into religious or medical rituals they began creating legends of their magical properties property, properties and powers.

Here are some interesting legends and myths concerning semi-precious and precious stones.

AMETHYST. Perhaps the most well-known myth about a crystal originates from Greece and is about Amethyst. The term "amethyst" is from the Greek meaning "amethystus" and means "drunken or drunk" ("methyein" also known as drunk as well as "methy" (also known as wine).

According to the legend, Dionysus, the god of celebration, wine as well as joviality and intoxication was furious with mortals and took revenge by having his 2 fierce tigers gobble up any mortal who crossed his path. There was a gorgeous young virgin called Amethysta who was heading to Diana's temple in order to honor the goddess. The god of vengeance unleashed his hungry tigers on her. Amethysta was crying out to Diana to get assistance. When Diana knew what was to happen she transformed Amethysta into a sculpture of sparkling clear quartz, thus shielding Amethysta from being snatched by tigers. When Dionysus was aware of what he had done, and was filled with regret the king began to cry in wine on the sculpture. His tears stained the statue of quartz to a deep purple, which led to the formation of Amethyst, the rock. Amethyst.

PERIDOT. Peridot was believed by some to possess the ability to dispel evil spirits. The name derives directly from it being the Arabic phrase "farodat" which means "gem". The early Egyptian priests were known to drink the stimulating drink known as Soma in cups made of peridot believing that it could draw them closer to Isis who was the goddess of the natural world and magic. This stone was believed to sparkle when dark and that's why miners were believed to have sought it at night and then marked their locations, returning in the dawn of day to recover the gems. Numerous stunning examples of peridot were returned from the Mediterranean region in the Crusades and were used to embellish European cathedrals, and they remain today.

RUBY. Ruby has been the most valuable gemstone for hundreds of years. It was believed to be among the valuable among the twelve stones. The term "ruby" is derived directly from Latin "ruber" which means red. It is believed that the ruby's sparkle is caused by an unstoppable internal fire which makes the stone a symbol of eternal love. Because of its strength and durability it's the perfect gemstone to make rings for engagements. If worn in the left hand, it is believed to bring good luck to the wearer.

Rubies were believed to be a symbol of the power and warmth. The ancient tribes used them to make ammunition for blowguns and even it was believed that an unheated pot of water could quickly boil if a stone was dropped into it. The ruby was ground into powder and then put on the tongue, rubies were used to treat for digestion issues (it also added "fire" to aid digestion). The wearer of a ruby believed to have a good health as well as wealth, wisdom, and love success. According to the Bible there's a passage that states that "wisdom is more valuable that rubies".

Today, diamonds are more valuable and rarer than the highest quality diamonds that are colorless! A 16 carat diamond was auctioned off at auction at Sotheby's for $227,300 in 1988.

TURQUOISE. Turquoise is named so because it was first brought to Europe by Turkey.

Turquoise was thought as a sacred stone, protecting against all forms of illness and evil. It was believed that the Egyptians used to mine turquoise from the Sinai at the time of 5,500 BC. The turquoise's blue color was believed to possess profound metaphysical properties according to numerous ancient civilizations. (It was believed to be the colour of the skies and which is the origin of all rain.) In the early days of Mexico turquoise was reserved for gods and was not worn by mortals. In Asia it was believed that turquoise as a powerful shield against evil eyes. In Tibet still to this day, turquoise is the most well-known of materials for personal ornamentation and is still used as an important role in religious ceremonies. Another theory was that turquoise was able to shield the wearer from injury resulting from falls (especially being thrown off a horse) and also helped the horse be more secure to be on his feet.

A gift of turquoise is a symbol of goodwill and fortune.

The story of Native American folklore, the Pima was believed to be a symbol of prosperity and strength. It was also believed it was believed that it could help overcome illnesses.

The Zuni believed that turquoise protected them from evil spirits.

In Hopi mythology, there is an lizard that travels in between below and excretes turquoise.

The Apache believed that attaching turquoise to weapons would increase the accuracy of the weapon. They also believed that wearing turquoise could prevent falling and breaking bones, and that wearing turquoise in a horse's bridle, or on its mane would guarantee that the horse's safety.

The Pueblos believed that the color turquoise was taken from the sky.

The Navajos believed they were blessed by rainfall by throwing down a chunk of turquoise into the river and praying to the gods of rain.

HEMATITE. It is a kind of iron ore that is among the most well-known grounding stones. In prehistoric times, it was used to create red ocher to paint caves. The early Egyptians employed hematite in amulets. Some were prescribed to combat inflamation and madness. Pliny was the first Roman historian, believed that hematite brought luck to those who wore it when they made a petition to the king, or requested a favorable ruling in a court. Today, hematite is advised for those who are in difficult legal issues.

It is believed that the Native Americans used hematite to make red and ocher face-paint. They used it as a war paint, believing it made them invincible during battle. They believed that it would make them invincible during battle. Romans also believed that it could make warriors immortal, as well as increasing their the strength and courage. The stone was crushed and then rubbed the powder onto their bodies.

TOPAZ. It was said that golden topaz changes color there was poisoned drinks or food and thus was the preferred stone for many royals and giving people the title imperial.

CLEAR QUARTZ. The Ancients believed that quartz crystals were an ice-like substance. The Greeks identified it as "crystallos" which means "frozen". The belief remained up to the 16th century, when scientists believed that it was fossilized Ice.

This crystal was used extensively in many the world's cultures:

It is among the seven precious elements of Buddhism;

It was set on the breastplates in the breastplate of Jesus, the Hebrew high priest of the Bible;

It was a stone of strength of shamans.

In the oldest written works on the planet that is the Sanskrit literature from the time of India Quartz crystals are known as Bhisma-Ratna. It means "the gemstone that eliminates anxiety".

RHODOCHROSITE. The Incas believed that rhodochrosite the stone they referred to as Inca Rose is the blood of previous queens and kings, which they turned into stone.

OPAL. A Australian Aboriginal legend tells how an opal and a pelican caused a firestorm to the locals. A few days ago the Wangkumara people were able to decide to send a Pelican in Northern Territory. Northern Territory so when it returned, it could inform them what was on the ground. The bird flew off with everything it needed to fish as well as water that it needed for the trip put in the pouch on his beak. After a time of flying and then deciding to be able to land on the an incline to relax. The bird looked down at the ground below him and was awestruck of the stunning colors in the rocks that lay at his feet. The rock he saw was opal. It was enthralled by the different colors of stones that it began to scratch at them using his beak. At once, sparks shot out and settled in the grassy area near. The flames slowly grew and started to spread across the hill toward the camp of Wangkumara near the bottom of the hill. The first time ever, the campers were able to cook their fish and meat and were happy with this new opportunity.

Chapter 6: The Application of Crystals

Uqsing crystal bracelets are a effective way to make use of this incredible collection of crystals. There are many options that you'll find an item that is suitable for your requirements. Wearing beautiful quartz jewelry, such as the smokey quartz crystal pendant that is that is shown below is an excellent option for jewelry.

Other types of quartz with outstanding metaphysical properties that help to keep them within your body are pink quartz crystals, Prasiolite often referred to as amethyst crystals with green color, yellow Citrine crystals, and Amethyst purple crystals.

Quartz crystals allows you to continuously make use of the protective and grounding energy they release. A stunning pendant, bracelet as well as a natural crystal necklace is an energizing energy. The smoky quartz crystals can be an extremely useful quartz crystal to utilize. Utilizing any of these natural crystals, whether it's the form of a pendant, a ring or any other type of jewelry, keeps the crystals in their sphere and creates the healing effects of quartz crystal. Because the earth naturally emits the smoky quartz, it could aid cancer patients who undergo radiation therapy. The pendants and necklaces made of the smoky quartz and tourmaline Quartz can be powerful tools to protect your psychic and shield you from negative energies and to strengthen your spiritual foundation They are great assets.

If the jewelry isn't worth it for you, then you could make use of a small piece of any quartz crystal by keeping it in your purse throughout the daytime. When they are in your own aura and energy, they can benefit you. Make sure you perform one of the cleaning procedures of your crystals on a regular basis. Quartz crystals are simpler than cleaning other crystals therefore, make sure you do it often to maintain your energy levels. This is also a good time to clean your crystal jewelry.

What is the best way to heal with crystals? Can Help You?

The healing properties of quartz crystals help to release negative energy and promote positive emotions and thoughts. There are a variety of quartz crystals that you could choose to test. The quartz amplifier property can transmit the energy of any kind of crystal you've selected to the place in which you are.

It is possible to purchase quartz that is carved into crystal skulls. To heal on spiritual levels they're extremely effective. Quartz crystal can also be used to create glass pendulums, glass bowls and crystal wands that are used to treat. Nature-based Lemurian crystal wands can also be amazing tools for healing. You should think about using quartz crystals if haven't already. It's easy to find and inexpensive to purchase. You'll be pleasantly surprised by how wonderful amethyst crystals feel or how the rose quartz crystal feel in your space.

Are you still pondering whether to heal by using Crystals?

Crystal therapy is a long-standing practice, and is commonly known as healing stones. The practice is considered to be an alternative healing method and people who adhere to it believe that the use of crystals and stones are able to treat ailments as well as other illnesses. Crystal therapy was developed in ancient times to regulate the chakras and transform the energies in the body creating an energetic field that is clear and clean. This healing method that is natural is used to help relax and alleviate anxiety.

Chapter 7: Crystals for Stress-Relief

What can I do with crystals to ease Stress?

If your body is under extreme stress your body's natural defenses are weakening which makes you more susceptible to developing mental, physical and emotional disorders. Stress reduction is an essential role in maintaining your health and prolonging your lifespan. The most effective option is to utilize healing crystals prior to any illness has a chance to be manifested.

Relaxation and Stress Relief Crystal Pattern for the Chakras

If you are aware of the chakras' location It should be simple to follow this process.

What you'll require:

4 Clear Quartz

3 Amethyst

2 Black Onyx

1 Rose Quartz

Make sure you are lying in a comfortable and comfortable position.

Then, place one amethyst over the third eye chakra. The one amethyst you choose should be placed on your palm on the right side of your hand, while the other one should be placed in the left side of your hand. Its function is to help you ground yourself and bring you to a state of calm. Additionally, the position the crystals are crucial in directing the energy upwards to your crown chakra, and afterwards, back down to the base chakra.

Then, place one onyx in the bottom of your left foot, and the other to the left sole. The goal of this exercise is to remove and eliminate negative energy out of your body which can cause stress.

Put the gemstone on your stomach. This is necessary to keep a harmony between male and female energies we all have. Additionally, you can place one of the crystals on your stomach, just below your rose quartz.

The second quartz crystal is to be laid over your head. The third should be placed beside your right side. Then, place the other to the side on your left. The reason for these crystals is crystals of clear quartz is to aid in cleansing the chakra and detoxifying the aura.

Once you're finished you'll have successfully created energy zones in two triangles through the position of crystals.

Release your muscle. Keep your eyes closed. Focus on your breathing.

Relax in a state of meditation for at least 10 minutes , or longer if you want.

After the event is over and you're done, you can make use of these crystals as stone of worry. Put them inside a silk pouch and carry them wherever you travel. When you start to feel the typical symptoms of anxiety starting to creep into your life, simply go into your pocket or purse, gently massage the stones of worry using your fingertips, and take strength from them.

What can I do to lessen stress and anxiety within the Workplace?

One of the primary reasons to use healing crystals is to assist people cope with the stresses of life. Although it's not possible to completely stay away from the stressors of life but healing crystals can reduce the negative effects they have on you body, mind, your emotions , and even your spirit.

The following stone are highly recommended to reduce stress at work. They also assist in increasing productivity. They also assist in smoothing your professional relations.

If you're looking for career success you should consider purchasing an Emerald. It is frequently utilized to draw the most abundance. It can also assist you in attaining mental clarity, thereby aiding you in understanding your objectives. Place this on the desk, and utilize it as a mental tool during your brief office breaks.

Many people struggle to establish appropriate boundaries for their professional relationships. This means that they are abused or given less respect than they merit. In such situations, keeping an amber crystal in your home is advised.

If you're not happy with the situation at your workplace and want to push to make a change, you can carry amethyst along with you. It will inspire courage and strength. it, so that you are able to handle a stressful workplace situation.

For those suffering from low productivity A garnet is recommended. It not only increases your productivity, but also those of your team members or your subordinates.

If communication isn't your forte Then the blue lace agate might prove extremely beneficial. It will help you communicating your thoughts effectively to your bosses, clients and colleagues. It is also a good choice for those who feel they're viewed as not appreciated and misunderstood.

Larimar is a different stone that works in clearing the way for communication. If you are struggling to communicate with others, utilize this crystal.

If you work at a computer for the entire day you should consider installing a purple fluorite in front of it. This will ensure that you're protected from the damaging consequences of the computer's electromagnetic field.

Are you being abused by someone who is stealing from your work environment? Does your boss suck up your spirit? Are your toxic coworker making you fall to the ground with them? If that's the case, you should carry an smoky quartz. This crystal will stop emotional vampires from draining every ounce of energy. If someone at work has been causing you to lose your self-esteem This crystal can aid in building confidence in yourself.

Figure 3: The Quartz can shield you from emotional vampires.

Source:

If you're getting stuck it's a good idea to use a bloodstone for stimulating your creative juices. It also aids in increasing the motivation you have to be productive. In addition, if you'd like to increase your ability to solve problems have an emerald.

Missing meetings? Having difficulty remembering deadlines? The rainbow obsidian can help, especially if you're looking to sharpen your memory.

Utilizing Crystals to aid in Psychic Healing

It is possibly the most effective, yet simple methods of healing your self and others through the use of crystals.

Choose a quiet and safe place.

Place the crystal you want to use before you. If, for instance, you're struggling with recovering from an addiction to alcohol, then you should make use of a Kunzite.

Examine the hue that the stone has. It has a soft pink hue. Imagine the glowing pink light emanating through the crystal, becoming larger and bigger until it's enough to cover the person you are (or the person you're trying to assist).

Through your imagination visualize your self (or your loved one you're helping) being embraced by the protective sheath of color. Look at its brilliance. Feel the warmth. Within the cloak of light You are safe and strengthened.

Chapter 8: What to Utilize Crystals

To Heal

There are many ways that you could harness the healing power of crystals and use them to your benefit. This chapter will discuss some of these methods, and also some helpful tips.

Programm the Crystal with Your Intention

Programming your crystal empowers it with the power needed to focus its healing abilities on the specific goal you've got in the back of your mind. The programming of your crystals in accordance with your desired intention helps increase the power of your crystal. Additionally, part of the program involves dedicating the stone to a god-like power (god or goddess, god or the power of the universe) to ensure that the power of the crystal's function can be increased. Use the steps below in order to programme your gemstone

* Ensure that the crystal is cleaned and cleared with an appropriate method from the one listed in chapter four.

Hold the crystal with your fingers and feel the power and energy. Following the cleansing process you will see it to be much more powerful and powerful than it was before. It is clear to feel the power of this crystal.

When you feel and experience this mystical and intrinsic power of the crystal pray to God or whatever god you trust to bring you closer to the crystal. Be aware that crystals behave like living things and are able to listen and react to demands regardless of whether the channel you are using is not one that you're familiar with.

* When you feel that connection to the core in the crystal shut your eyes and visualize the intention you wish to give it power. Imagine the outcome in your head and visualize that a white streak that is streaming out of this image, that is moving toward the crystal. Then, imagine this image covering every corner and nook of the crystal until your intention is fully enclosed within the crystal.

* Now, close your eyes slowly and say a prayer of thanks to the crystal for allowing it to assist you with your issues. The crystal is programmed to energy that is based on your intentions. You are able to draw the energy of your crystal whenever you wish to achieve your goals.

Another important step in programming your stone should be to dedicate the stone to ensure that nobody else is able to reprogram it either intentionally or accidentally. These are the steps to dedicate your gemstone that you have programmed to your angel of protection for security:

* Hold the crystal with the program in your hands and exclaim"May only the highest-energy energy in the universe make use of this crystal and the energy it emits.'

* Focus your attention on your crystal in a concentrated manner until you are convinced that your angelic guardian has heard your request and accepted your request.

* The crystal has been secured and is protected from abuse.

Meditation with Crystals

One of the greatest difficulties with meditation is that it's extremely simple to comprehend and requires nothing apart from your body and mind but it could take a life time. But, there are tools that could help accelerate progress in learning to meditate and can help you attain higher levels of meditation that you had before. The healing power of crystals is one of the tools that boosts the effectiveness of meditation. Utilize the following methods to meditate using crystals:

Choose your gemstone. Numerous factors must be considered in order in making the best decision. Some of the components that have to be considered in your crystal selection are:

This is the frequency you use to describe your personal vibratory energy; select the crystal that aligns to this frequency.

* Your purpose should be clear; choose a crystal the crystal that aligns with your goals. Read Chapters Five and Six in order to know which crystal is the best for what purpose before making your decision.

There are times when you may need to choose an item that amplifies the strength of the particular gemstone you've picked according to the properties. As an example, if you've chosen rose quartz for its ability to draw romantic love into your life, you can place the crystal in one hand and hold clear quartz or selenite in the opposite hand so that the qualities associated with rose quartz get magnified.

Find a place that is suitable to meditate. It should be silent and quiet. If you decide to set up an area in your home and you want to be sure that all electronic devices are turned off or switched to silent mode so that they aren't a nuisance.

Place the crystals with your fingers and repeat your intentions. Let that the energy from the stones to move throughout your body as you gently hold the crystals. Visualize your goals resulting in positive outcomes in your thoughts and let the healing light of the crystal to illuminate the image of your goal. Just place your trust in your crystals and ask their assistance without hesitation. Crystals attract you because they are eager to assist you.

Close your eyes and pay attention to your breathing. Take note of the flow and outflow that your breathing makes. When your mind wanders elsewhere, slowly return your attention to your breathing.

You can mentally scan your body and ease tension from areas that are feeling stressed.

Imagine the energy of the crystals that flow out of your palms and circulating throughout your body, rejuvenating and reviving every cell.

There is no restriction to this session. It is possible to sit for all you want to. When you're content with your experience take a moment to open your eyes slowly and be grateful to the universal power as well as your angelic guardian as well as the crystal for taking part in the meditation along with you.

Designing Healing Grids or Layouts

They are efficient instruments that can help you manifest your desires, goals and dreams. The major difference between one crystal and a crystal grid is it is made up of a latticed energy system which combines energies of several crystals to achieve the highest results. Alongside the energy fields of a variety of crystals, the grid can also utilizes the power of geometrical figures and your intent obviously.

The strength of the sacred geometry as well as numerous crystals will magnify your ideas to no end, giving you much enhanced results than just one crystal could. The drawback is that you can't make crystal grids that are ready for immediate use, which is why a single crystal is the best choice. Therefore, based on your needs, you can pick between a crystal and an underlying crystal grid to draw the power and the energy of gems. The following steps to make the crystal grid or layout:

Items needed to construct a gridare:

* A suitable, undisturbed location in your home

* A tiny note with your intentions clearly written on it

* A central stone which is extremely effective in directing your intent more effectively than if had a grid that did not have a central stone

* Stones that have energy fields that are synchronized with your intent

The quartz crystal is used used to be activated by the grid

A cloth that is used to lay across the grid of crystals although this is not required and it is possible to make a grid using the floor or table, the majority of healers agree it is a good idea to use a fabric because it increases the effectiveness for the grid.

The first step to creating a crystal grid is to be aware of your goal and understanding. What's the goal for your crystal grid? Do you wish to eliminate negative energy? Do you wish to bring good luck and prosperity to your life? Do you want to increase your level in your creative abilities?

* Determine your goal and write down it on the small scrap of paper. The choice of your goal is crucial as it will influence the choice of crystals. For instance, if you're seeking abundance and wealth and prosperity, then you should pick a crystal that is 'wealth' such as citrine, pyrite, aventurine and so on. But, keep in mind that there isn't a proper or incorrect crystals that you can pick from. Be awed by your intuition and choose the gemstones you find appealing.

Cleanse the area on the which you plan to build your grid by smudging it with Sage or using any other cleansing procedure that is discussed in Chapter Four.

* Fold the sheet on which you've written your particular goal. Put it in the middle on the cloth grid.

Now, close your eyes, take a deep breath and then state your intent loudly. Alternately you could imagine your goal in your head.

Then, begin placing the crystals on the paper, with your intentions written on the paper. Begin from the outermost layer then move towards the inside until you get to the paper. Be sure to keep your goal while placing each stone on the grid.

Finally, put the crystal in the center of the piece of paper with the written message.

It is the next thing to do activating the grid with Quartz crystal points. To do this, grab this crystal. Draw imaginary lines that connect all the crystals in the grid. The process connects the crystals energetically to one another. It's like playing that game for kids known as 'connect the dots'.

Through this process your grid will be was activated and its healing energy has begun to work. To increase the energy that your grid has you can put candles or other tools for enhancing energy on the grid.

Making Crystal Elixirs and Essences

The creation and use of gem essences is a wonderful method for gaining the healing properties of a particular crystal. The crystal is then placed into clean water. The highly vibrated water allows it to absorb gemstone's meanings as well as the healing properties of the crystal. They can provide the body with revitalizing energy. The water is similar to mineral springs that were utilized for centuries for healing both internally and externally. Gem essences are designed to help stabilize the energy centers in your body.

Gem essences are easy making at-home. When selecting the crystals that you use to create the essences of gems it is suggested to select stones with similar significance and properties, to ensure that the intention behind the healing stones is identical. For example, if you wish to bring the energy of love into your life the first thing that a person will consider is the beautiful flower of one that resembles love. With this in mind it is possible to make a Rose Quartz essence. It is important to thoroughly clean the crystal prior to using it or making any crystal essence in order to rid it of any toxins and negative energies.

The procedure to make crystal essence is relatively easy. You'll need an open glass jar preferably with a lid , and the crystals that are fully exposed to the full moon or the sun. The exposure cleans the crystals and prepares them to use.

Begin by holding your crystals with both hands and then state your intention. The intention could be visualized or stated out loud. You can also state the benefits that you would like to reap following the process of healing crystals out loud. By doing this, you can transmit the intention from the crystal directly to the essence. It is possible to seek guidance from God and practice a variety of breathing exercises to cleanse the mind of all negative thoughts and help in the healing process.

The crystals should be placed at within the container's bottom, and add pure water (preferably the alkaline). Cover the lid of the glass jar and set the entire arrangement to the sunlight for 2 to 4 hours for it to recharge. The jar could be left out for up to 24 hours, so that the essence gets all the sunlight and moonlight. However, this approach could be hazardous when the chosen crystals contain components that, if utilized in excess, can cause poisoning. It is suggested that you put the remaining elixir into the refrigerator.

After this Be cautious around crystals. If you are spending too much time in their presence or make any kind of direct bodily contact with them may interfere with the stone, and this diminishes the overall healing effects.

There are a variety of methods that one can make use of the essence that the one he has made. Many people prefer to apply some drops directly on their necks, on their skin or even inside their tongues every day. Some prefer to mix it in drinks that they drink throughout the day, so that they get the essentials at certain times.

For maximum benefit It is suggested that the essence be blended with body lotion that is used when bathing. This way they are cleaned externally and internally. To get a good start to the day, people place their essence into bottles with spritzers and then spray it on their faces when they wake up.

The essence of rose quartz is known to open one's heart to happiness, love and forgiveness. It makes people more compassionate and welcoming, while also balancing emotions, bringing peace and harmony within.

Benefits of using Crystal Essence - Various advantages are derived from consuming various crystal essences. For instance Quartz crystals can be used to store, concentrate, and amplify energy. They also help to increase spiritual development and wisdom. Moonstone Moonstone is a personal stone, and can bring the success you desire in business and love matters. It is considered as the one most powerful and efficient when the moon is full. Moonstone can help receive guidance through the unconscious mind in order to bring a person to a calm state and regulate their mood.

Pink Tourmaline is believed to bring peace, acceptance and peace towards oneself. Its effects are known as "Aphrodisiac", named for the Greek god who is the love of all, Aphrodite. It is believed that it transforms negativity into positivity. Desert Rose Selenite helps in getting rid of negative energies.

Ametrine can be very beneficial to treat long-lasting and long-lasting ailments because it makes the patient to the root of the disease. It also aids to reduce stress and boosts creativity. Blue Aragonite can be useful in encouraging patience in people and people who are too self-critical. It helps balance emotions and clears any obstructions that may be in the throat or heart.

Amethyst is extensively used to promote spiritual development and to reduce addiction to alcohol and drugs. Lepidolite is a particular remedy to alleviate stress and depression and it is thought to create an optimistic future for those who purchase.

The Tibetan Quartz crystal is among twelve Master crystals because it is extremely potent. It aids in recalling dreams and can help a person to meditate. It is also known as the "feel good' stone since it boosts physical strength, energy and endurance.

Blue Lace Agate is a stone with a gentle energy. It creates a cool and peaceful impact. Its primary purpose is to promote tranquility. Alongside its cooling effect it also reduces anger, resentment and anxiety. If you're facing an intense battle, whether either in your professional or personal life, it's recommended to take in this essence Blue Lace Agate to go well-prepared for what lies ahead. It can also help individuals to know more about him and her.

Prehnite is a crystal essence that is used to boost spiritual development. It assists in visualize what they desires. It can be beneficial for long-term meditation. To rid yourself of any painful or negative previous experiences, people consume essential oils of this stone in order to "clean their minds to be able to move forward,

Create a sacred Space within Your Home

You can make use of the energy crystals by making a sacred space or altar at home. Indeed sacred spaces at homes are becoming more popular because a large number of people utilize the sacred space to practice their yoga or meditate with no disturbance.

The creation of a sacred space within your home with crystals will serve as a reminder to keep moving towards your goal every time you take an glance or walk through the space. It is possible to create an adobe grid of crystals in your space of sacredness, and then reorganize the grid every when you wish to have a fresh purpose to achieve it using their power.

Alternative ways of using crystals

It is easy to carry the crystals you love in your bag or pocket. Be aware that certain gemstones are extremely soft and brittle and, if handled them in a reckless manner it could cause damage to them.

Add crystals in your bath to allow the healing properties to soak into your body via the pores of your skin. However that not all crystals are suitable to be placed in water, so, make sure to study before adding any stone to your bathwater.

You can place the crystals that provide energy anywhere in your home, including your living room, bedroom and study areas, kitchen or even your office. Here are some suggestions of the best crystal to use in which space:

The crystals you can use for bedroom Three crystals that work well for bedrooms are amethyst, black tourmaline and, of course, rose quartz. The energy of the auric field in each of these stones help to create affection, intimacy, and a better relationship with your partner.

Crystals for the living space Living room crystals Selenite is an excellent crystal to use in the living room as is the apophyllite. While this book doesn't provide a detailed explanation but it's sufficient to be aware that both apophyllite and selenite encourage transparency, openness, and transparency so that families can be close without worry or doubt.

Crystals for the kitchen If there's a single crystal that's ideal to be used in your kitchen it should be carnelian because of its capacity to stimulate the capacity for creativity by opening the sacral chakra. No other room within the home requires creativity more than your kitchen since you are required to cook nutritious and tasty meals for your family on a regular basis.

Crystals to decorate the dining room Crystals for the dining area Turquoise is a wonderful crystal to put in the dining room because it aids in the development of healthy and healthy eating habits. Citrine is placed within the dining space assists in bringing your dining area and dining experience with joy and happiness.

Crystals for office spaces - Make use of pyrite for your office area or office to gain focus and clarity of mind to ensure that you make informed decisions that will positively influence your professional decision-making skills and decisions.

Finally, you can create beautiful jewelry using your favourite crystals and put them around your body. In addition, you gain have access to the healing properties of crystals but you also enhance your physical appearance by adding some oomph and grace to your appearance.

The healing properties that crystals possess can be used in many ways. You are able to choose the best method based on the availability of space, the ease of use, as well as other aspects that are specific to your personal lifestyle and requirements.

Chapter 9: 50 Crystals to Be aware
of (From A to Z)

Aegirine

The stunningly beautiful gemstone ranges from deep to dark green in color and is believed to have extremely powerful energy that protects. By securing the chakra system, physical body and aura during times of danger and difficult times, Aegirine has earned its reputation as a stone that instills confidence, courage and conviction to those who feel its light, cool energy. Most commonly, it is located within Canada, Greenland, Russia, Scotland, and Nigeria, Aegirine as a name originates of Aegirine, which is the name of the Norse sea goddess Aegir and is known as Acmite due to the Greek word meaning "point" which is a fitting description because Aegirine is usually seen sticking out of rocks like blades that protrude from the earth. Aegirine is an excellent crystal to help overcome self-consciousness as well as the unnecessary guilt that comes from facing the harsh judgments of others about our appearance or lifestyle choices.

Agate

Agate is a common name used to describe a variety of types of Chalcedony which show an unlimited array of colours pure mixed, banded, or colorless. Also known as the 'earth rainbow The belief is it Agate as well as its extensive color spectrum is the symbol of the various state of our innermost universe. Agate has a lower vibrational frequency than the majority of gemstones nevertheless, its energy is extremely powerful in balancing the aura. It it has a stabilizing effect that helps to increase responsibility, stability, and maturity, and also serves as an incredible channel for spiritual energy that results in self-confidence and confidence in yourself.

Amazonite

Amazonite is a beloved stone with stunning shades of green and turquoise and, upon first contact, is believed to soothe the mind and replenish the soul. It is sometimes referred to as the stone of Courage and Truth' Amazonite empowers the individual on a path of self-discovery that leads to the discovery of one's own truths. The calming energy it provides tempers unruly emotions and helps to remove any emotional blockages or traumas from the past that are accumulating in the body's energy network. Amazonite is excellent for cleaning and resetting chakras; it connects our physical bodies and the ethereal that dissolves inner conflicts it helps focus efforts and to enhance the results. Amazonite is also a great way to enhance and balance the link between the intellect (mind) as well as intuition (heart) giving a balanced resonance that can lead to improved capabilities and greater clarity.

126

Amber

Amber has since Neolithic times, been among the most sought-after gems of the world and this is not just due to its stunning warmth which is similar to honey in golden hue, but as well because it was regarded as an offering from the sea. Amber is a Greek term Anbar was coined around the time of 14th century to describe the term used to describe what we refer to as Ambergris (ambergris or gray amber) that is a waxy resin that is made by sperm whales. It is used in a variety of the highest-end perfumes as well as scents. In the 15th century the word "amber" was widened and included Baltic amber (yellow amber) that is a fossilized (usually in the case of trees) sap or resin and takes thousands of years to create.

Amethyst

Amethyst, a semi-precious kind of Quartz crystal that can be found in various locations all over the world. It typically is found in shades ranging from pale pink/violet to a deep blue and purple Sometimes, it appears to have red-colored secondary shades. The name Amethyst originates from the word ametusthos, a geeky word that means "not drunk" and through time it has been praised for its unique benefit of preventing excessive drinking and drunkenness. It is believed that wearing an Amethyst pendant around the navel will bring the sense of sobriety and control over excessive thoughts. Keeping Amethyst in your pocket can boost your intelligence and encourage smart business decisions.

Apatite

Apatite was named an origin from the Greek word meaning 'deceive in a way', mostly due to the range of various colors Apatite selects to display. Apatite is an incredibly multifaceted gem that is generally blue but can also be brown, yellow and green. Apatite has many beneficial properties like helping the body absorb calcium, which improves the strength of bones, cartilage teeth, joints, and aids in addressing issues related to hypertension.

Aquamarine

The name comes in it's Latin aqua Marinus which translates to "water of the sea" Aquamarine has been used for centuries by sailors to protect themselves at sea. This soothing stone with its shades of green and blue is a symbol of the pure and clearness of crystal waters, with profound connections to truth, trust and revelation. is utilized as a tool for meditation acts as a mirror, revealing secrets of reality and even our own inner levels.

Aventurine

Aventurine crystals are gems which contain a good amount of Quartz as well as other mineral inclusions that work together to provide Aventurine its diverse colours. The different mineral inclusions affect not only the colour of the stone but also its energies, connections, and healing properties. The name comes from the Italian Ventura, which means "by chance," and is commonly associated with luck. It is also called the 'Stone of Opportunity'.

Bloodstone

The Ancients recognized Bloodstone as Heliotrope which is derived from two Greek words that mean'sun-turning and believed to safeguard the body and mind of wearers and is long used as a symbol of vital longevity and health. This stone that has been known to improve mental acuity and to ward against illnesses such as colds and flu through energizing the entire body system. It also can boost overall endurance.

Carnelian

Carnelian is a mineral that is found in India and South America and exists in colors of red and orange, with dark reds being most sought-after. Carnelian is recognized to be one of the rocks that promote motivation , and has strong links to physical strength and courage that can aid introverts and shy people in assuming the leadership positions and becoming more engaging and articulate public speaking. The name carnelian originates from the Latin word for flesh. It was in Ancient Egypt, Carnelian was called 'the sun setting due to its orange color containing female energy frequencies, with red stones being linked to male energy.

Citrine

Citrine's name originates in it being derived from the French word citron which means "lemon" but it is also known as The Merchant's Stone due to its incredible ability to increase balances in banks, as well as it is also known as the Stone of the Mind due to the old belief that the placing of the Citrine Stone on your forehead will stimulate the user's psychic abilities. Natural Citrine is pure and glowing yellow color, with sometimes transparent golden hues that emit energy-producing frequencies that neutralize negativity and produce an atmosphere that attracts only the most positive and most joyful of moods.

Diamond

Also referred to as also known as Crystal of Light or the King of Stones, Diamonds are undoubtedly the most well-known and most well-known gemstone. Diamond has strong ties to winter, and as an winter stone, with its ice-like color and clarity and has a higher frequency of energy than normal, which could be the reason why it is considered to be the most durable gemstone on Earth.

Fluorite

The stone of Positivity", for reasons that aren't known, does not get the attention that some of the famous stones, but this doesn't mean it's any less attractive or powerful. Fluorite comes in a variety of colors and is regarded as the most vibrant stone. Its most well-known shades include shades of purple and blue as well as oranges, reds, browns, blacks and greens, as well as transparent, and any combination of these. capabilities related to manifestation as well as creativity and magic.

Garnet

Garnet is a stone of balance that is typically found in Africa but is also found throughout both the United States and Russia, this red-colored gemstone is a long-standing symbol of love, compassion and purity. It also offers a means to higher levels of spiritual understanding. Garnet comes in a variety of forms , including the red/brown Almandine (a stone of Tangible of Truth), Merelini Mint Garnet, and Carbuncle which is the most sought-after is the precious or Noble Garnet. This precious stone is believed to enhance the wearer's capacity to manifest real and positive in the world of psychic perception.

Hematite

Hematite is used since the time in the time of the early Greeks who utilized it to make vibrant blood-red dyes. Natural Hematite (when refined) exhibits an iridescent silvery sheen , believed to be awe-inspiring to the person who holds it similarly to the moonlight at night. Hematite is an essential component to any collection of healers. It is a rich iron content that is believed to boost circulation, blood pressure and heart health and relieve menstrual cramps.

Jade

Jade is also known as the "Dream stone" is a powerful connection to the spiritual realm, which allows a skilled user of gemstones to gain insights into the old-fashioned knowledge that is both occult and ritualistic (beware-this isn't always an excellent thing). Another stone is visible to us in a myriad of vibrant shades, with many having their own unique connections, energies that are healing, protective and healing characteristics, yet is usually believed to be green gem. Since the beginning of time, it has been believed that Jade is a blessing to all it comes into contact with its energy of peace and purity.

Kyanite

Kyanite is an green, blue or black crystal that is renowned for its capabilities in high-speed energy transmission, communication, and connection and connection. It is most likely recognized for its ability to improve psychic abilities such as divination and telepathy. This is an essential stone for healers. Kyanite's high frequency energy instantly forms bonds between patients and healers, enhancing the healing effects and increasing the speed of healing. It is one of the two crystals that are not infected with negative energy, through the elimination of negative energy prior to any accumulation of negative energy can be created. It is the ideal stone to cleanse the other crystals (and rooms) of any negative energy.

Lapis Lazuli

Lapis Lazuli also known as 'The Stone of Truth It has been used since at least 4000bc . It was extensively used to embellish the sarcophagus of King Tutankhamun. It was not just valued because of its appearance, Lapis Lazuli was used for the production of the highly valuable and costly Ultramarine-based dyes, medicine, cosmetics.

Moonstone

Moonstone or "The Traveller's Stone' has strong connections to the moon, and its feminine energy. Most often, an opaque white sometimes with an ethereal sheen. Moonstone is also able to display elegant and subtle shades of pale blue, grey, and peach. Moonstone is used in jewelry for many thousands of years throughout the world, and has for a long time been linked to love, hope and reconciliation. Spiritually and emotionally Moonstones aids in the overcoming of issues of the ego, and decreases dependence on, and attachment to, unnecessary materialistic pursuits. It is believed that Moonstone can treat insomnia, sleepwalking as well as sleep paralysis, among other conditions related to sleep.

Obsidian

Usually, an opaque black gem Obsidian's color can vary from the darkest black to brown, and may be a host of diverse mineral inclusions which appear as white flecks like snow, or incandescent stripes of vivid blue violet, red gold, and green. Obsidian has been regarded as sacred stone since the beginning of time, and antique statues, relics, jewelry, amulets and even weapons that have sharp Obsidian instruments and blades have been discovered that date back to the Stone age. Black Obsidian is believed to aid the body's digestion and purging toxic substances, ease inflammation that cause joint pain, arthritis and accelerates the healing process of injuries and bruises. Obsidian is also able to absorb airborne pollutants and negative energy. However because of this amazing capability, it must be cleaned regularly by running it through cold water.

Onyx

Traditional Onyx are formed in thick black strips that are followed by thin white stripes , however it they can also show hues of brown, red and honey. Onyx is among the rare stones that are recognized as a stone of luck', however it has not led to it falling into negative repute. Onyx is a stone which boosts self-realisation as well as determination by providing an extra boost to manifest and realisation of dreams even though it's a bit like a contradiction stone, it does not diminish its benefits when utilized by a professional practitioner.

Peridot

Peridot (also known as Chrysolite is among the few stones that are formed in only one color green. The hues vary in dark, lime-green tones, to olive greens to lighter shades of yellowish-green, but they always remain within the'green' range which is the only pure lime green being the most sought-after. It is referred to in the eyes of those of the Romans as the "evening Emerald' because of its magnificent light-refracting properties, particularly when seen in the light of a candle. Peridot is also ascribed the reputation of being 'The Ultimate Gem' because of its uniqueness in the fact that (with Diamond being the only exception) Peridot is the sole gemstone that is not created within the crust of earth, but instead through the massive force and the molten rock flowing through the mantle of earth and is only transported to the surface through extreme events such as volcanic eruptions and earthquakes.

Quartz (clear)

Yet mysterious, this amazing gemstone is among the most plentiful and widely acknowledged gemstone in the world. Quartz is a gem that has been around for ages. Quartz family is huge It is part of the biggest family of the realm of mineral. Despite its abundance, Quartz was always highly prized, and there is a long-held conviction that Quartz is in reality living, and bridging the gap between mineral and animal and one that breathes only once every century.

Red Beryl (Bixbite)

Red Beryl's rareness makes it one of the most expensive gems in the world (as as high at $10.000 for a carat). It is often called Red Emerald, which is not correct since emerald is actually, a color and as a stone. Emerald is actually an green variant of Beryl. It is also known as the "Stone of the Right time' Red Beryl is said to lead the wearer to the right situations and provide assistance in guiding us in making the right choice. Like its name implies, Red Beryl carries a red color that ranges from deep and translucent reds of raspberry to light, almost pinkish shades.

Rose Quartz

It is a stone Of Unconditional Love' and has its name derived from its gorgeously subtle shades of pink. It emits a sense warmth and radiates a compassionate energy that, via its Heart Chakra, resonates deeply with the chakras in all their forms and serves to strengthen and nourish the body's energetic networks overall. Resentment and feelings of discontent are not able to manifest when through the energy that of Rose Quartz and negative feeling in a space that is filled by the vibrational energy of Rose Quartz can be squelched. It is a healing stone. Rose Quartz has been used to soothe burns, boost and sustain the health of your heartbeat, increase fertility, treat respiratory illnesses and also as an elixir. It is used to treat boils, wrinkles and blisters.

Ruby

Ruby is the color of Corundum that is red (other colors are also available, for instance blue, which are all Sapphires) It is also known as the "King of Gems and is considered to be among the top precious and sought-after stones around the globe. Rubies even outshined Diamonds in ancient times for their beauty, elegance, and opulence. Ruby has a profound impact in your Heart Chakra and protects it against the loss of energy. It also helps help balance the body's energy networks and aura.

Sapphire

Typically, royal blue Sapphire is a kind of corundum, similar to Ruby in every way, except colour (Rubies are actually red corundum) However the other color variants are all known as Sapphire. The gorgeous colours of Sapphire vary from Royal blue, to light blue yellow, orange and even purple. Sapphire is a very robust stone with numerous practical applications, besides being used to create beautiful jewelry and is long linked to royalty, prophecy and divinity across all religions. Sapphires have been coveted for their power to repel evil spirits, and to ward off and deflect curses and spells of evil, while also supercharging the powers of the person who wears it.

Selenite

The moon goddess is closely associated with Selene it is believed that if the moon's reflection is observed through the lens of a Selenite crystal, Selene herself is visible. The crystal's brightness is truly beautiful and is among the rare gemstones which need charging, but also possess the capability to purify and rejuvenate other crystals. This makes Selenite valued by healers, spiritualists as well as those who have mastered ancient wisdom. It is also known as the 'Stone Moon Goddess' as well as the "Master Stone The energy of Selenite is harmonious with the positive side of the of the earth's energetic field. It also serves as a conduit to the calm moon's energy and her numerous blessings.

Tourmaline

Tourmaline is a highly sought-after precious stone that is actually the most vivid of all stones. It is transparent or opaque and comes in all shades of clear and black, white violets, blues and browns, greens pinks, reds yellow or even multi-coloured. The range of value of Tourmaline is enormous, with basic stones like grey and black appearing low, especially in comparison to Paraiba which is a neon blue/green variety of Tourmaline that has an incandescent internal glow and can fetch thousands of dollars for a carat, making it among the most expensive gemstones on the planet.

Turquoise

Turquoise is thought to be the oldest gem that has been discovered by mankind. It is also the one that throughout history has been linked with the wisest of kings as well as the bravest warriors. It was also used to embellish the mask of death of Tutankhamun. It has been prized throughout the ages as a symbol of wisdom and knowledge of the past and also for its protective properties. Turquoise is the name given to it by its soft green and blue hues that it exhibits as well as being used to create sacred ornaments, amulets and talismans that bring luck and power for more than 7700 years. It is believed that Turquoise might be able to help guide, or even directly guide the adept shaman to the goal of eternal life.

Chapter 10: Answering a Few

Questions

Now that you are aware of crystals There are a several questions that need to be answered.

How do I purchase the stones from a reputable buyer?

There are a lot of crystals on the market. It is difficult to distinguish the genuine from fake ones is not easy. Therefore, it is recommended to read a book on crystals, such as this. There are many books on crystals online as well as articles on them. Understanding crystals can help you when purchasing crystals. Buying genuine crystals from shops that showcase crystals exactly as what they are will help you make a better selection. Some sellers of crystals will attempt to offer fake items However, don't be frightened. Be sure to ask any seller selling crystals until you're happy and you have earned the most value for your money.

You can use crystals instead of professional healthcare?

The answer is simple: no. It is certainly beneficial to look for alternative solutions however, ignoring the actual research and evidence-based methods is not the best way to go about attracting crystals also. They do have therapeutic properties, but they can't replace modern medical system. Also, crystals can't be substituted for medicine or medications.

Do you want to choose any crystal that you like and put it to use?

It is important to understand the distinction between stones and crystals. The most effective way to learn about crystals is to simply expand your knowledge, as mentioned previously. Learn about the nature of it, its healing properties as well as physical qualities.

Avoid using random crystals. They are also harmful because they contain toxin. It is ok to follow your gut However, it is important to know the facts prior to that. When you create crystal water, you need to be cautious when you make crystal water. Learn more about the subject prior to attempting any thing.

FAQ

Which are the most desirable stones? or polished?

If you can find an original stone, not polished or cut, choose them as they are authentic and are more vibrational. However there's no problem with polished crystals as well. Also, it's an issue of preference too. For instance, if you are using the original Selenite the stones easily break when they mimicked reflecting rubbles every time you get them in contact, therefore it's better to use polished Selenite.

Are you able to offer suggestions for those who aren't crystal-savvy?

Take a look at this book.

Are crystals acknowledged as a healing agent throughout the world?

Crystals are easily found throughout the globe today. This also shows how widespread they are. Crystals are also an integral part of a certain culture. Their importance in the past is astounding. It is possible to purchase crystals on the internet. There are many books and experts available on the market. You can conduct a search and learn more.

Do crystals' sizes matter in crystals?

The most straightforward answer is yes. Larger crystals have a higher vibratory frequency than smaller ones. However, this shouldn't devalue it that the smaller crystals don't have the power. They can be utilized in a variety of ways. From jewelry to carrying them in your pockets, there are methods to hold them close to you than more expensive crystals. However, they also come in larger sizes that can reach as high as six feet, but they aren't able to use them in a variety of ways.

What happens if you meet people who don't believe in crystals, can crystals do the work for them?

Crystals transmit vibration. They are able to sense your vibration and communicate with them. They can sense how you feel. If you don't trust that they are real, then they won't perform for you. It is important to feel and feel their energy. If you do not let them in and they don't offer their doors to you. If you want to receive their own vibration to heal The doors are always ready to them. If you don't believe in them, look for other ways to heal.

What do you think it means when someone is drawn to crystals?

This usually means that the crystal is meant for you. For certain people, crystals pop up in the middle of out of the blue. This is because their circumstances require that crystal to help their condition. When you visit an establishment, you will be able to take a look at the various crystals, one at a time, in your hands. Consider how you feel about them , and the ones that you are attracting yourself to.

If you have purchased crystals, what do you do with the crystals?

If you are making your first purchase take the crystals and soak them in salt water to rid them of any negative energy they've accumulated in the shop. You can then place those crystals into sunlight to recharge. Make use of the crystals by holding them to make your wishes manifest in them . This is similar to the mantras mentioned in this book.

Are crystals too costly?

The answer is simple: no. It's all up to you. The price of the crystal is determined by the type of stone as well as its source. There are three main types of crystals, and their prices differ between the three varieties. They are the raw stones, cut stones and tumblestones. Raw stones do not have a shine, however they have high-frequency vibration, whereas cut stones look like gemstones , and they are polished. They can be worn as jewelry. In contrast they are easily available. They don't require lots of money on tumblestones.

Do crystals have a expiry date?

Yes, you can recharge them by exposing them to sunlight, or make use of them during the full moon. They won't expire however they could become out of sync to the Mother Nature.

Chapter 11: Crystal Healing And

Your Health

Crystals have been adored for their beauty and therapeutic effects. The Melbourne Art Gallery clarify their geochemical origins and several rooms have been earmarked to display crystals. Through time, the practice of crystal healing has stood up to opposition from skeptical individuals, which is why it's somewhat comforting to know that the science of Geology regards them with such a high regard that they dedicate spaces in the museums crystals.

What I'm going to discuss is the possibility that crystal healing may be effective and attempt to shed some clarity on the reasons why some people experience a feeling of wellbeing and healing after an energy healing session with crystals.

To understand, Let's return to the science lab. We learned that everything is composed of atoms. Solids consist of a lot of moving atoms. They appear solid because the particles are so compact (close to one another) that they look solid. The most dense materials that contain atoms are even smaller in density and liquid is gas.

Actually, everything we see which includes me as well, is made up of tiny particles or atoms that have been oscillating (moving) however we are unable to detect that they are moving as our senses aren't able to detect the motion.

Crystals are also composed of atoms that are able to oscillate (move) in a particular speed. The research is done over the last 50 years or more at UCLA to investigate this issue and they are available on the internet.

The way your body moves, feels, think, etc. is uniquely yours. There's nobody else in this planet (which you have seen at this point) who is a copy of you.

We are influenced by the resonances of others If you're not convinced this, just listen for an hour someone you know on the phone who is feeling down. when they're done and you shut off the call, you're being down as well.

We are absorbing other people's vibrations and allowing people to connect with us through our energy. The same way crystals, as well as everything else around us vibrates with a particular frequency that is a characteristic of the rose quartz crystal topaz, and the like.

Crystals are distinctive because they possess a hierarchy of molecules that are distinct and vibrate (vibrate) differently. This makes crystals distinct from the name e.g. Smokey quartz is different from amethyst. This can cause a difference when they come in close contact with each of us.

Our vibration starts to shift because the crystal is close to us and we will be more influenced by those by the crystals around us.

This is an aspect of the research I mentioned earlier , and it is readily accessible on the internet. It is said that because crystals interact with our vibrations. crystals have a positive influence on our energy centers, and the way the atoms of our bodies oscillate change.

If you study the literature on the properties of each crystal, there's a wealth of information related to how they might affect you and how each crystal is able to heal different emotions as well..

There's evidence enough to prove this to be true. people feel better after having had a crystal healing.

Some people may not think they are thinking, there is reasons why people have different feelings. Take all the research, and it's possible to be unsure whether it's just an effect of a placebo.

The healer applies crystals to be placed on or around the body or in the energy field. The client will usually lie down on a mattress or on the floor. The ideal conditions are when the room is dark; there are candles and some soothing music or fragrant incense.

The idea is that the client rests while the crystals work. The amount of time needed to complete the process is dependent on the level of recovery needed.

Crystals alter the manner in which energy centers, also known as chakras vibrate and remove blocks in energy and emotions in the energy field as well as the physical body.

The new energy can enter by removing these blocks, and will flow to improve health, life and vitality.

They are also a method to bring balance and healing to your body, thoughts and emotions as well as the soul. If it's right appropriate for you can be determined by the results and your own personal experience may be helpful if you test it yourself.

Don't think that two therapies or even one of them will do miracles. It's taken you several months, or even years, of neglecting specific parts of your life and there's no magic wand that can sweep it off. This is the reality not a show and healing requires time.

The use of crystals for healing ailments

The Crystal Therapy is an therapy which is used to provide relief from various ailments, such as anxiety and pain.

The fast-paced lifestyle and the long hours of work can cause conditions such as stress and body pain. This method can greatly help in bringing comfort. The therapy has been used from the beginning of time.

In the treatment of crystals the use of crystals and stones is frequently employed. The belief is that crystals aid in providing benefits of healing to our bodies.

Certain of the crystals and stones are believed to have curative properties. The crystals and stones are placed in an effective function to provide an impact.

This treatment for healing is basically an art. There isn't any scientific evidence for this treatment method.

It is often used for its relaxing effect. The crystals, when applied to the skin provide an energizing effect.

The reason for this treatment involves stimulating skin cells. The result is the release of hormones and enzymes that aid in promoting relaxation.

It is thought that the mom figure has a cure for a variety of illnesses. There are many materials that have the healing properties of.

The crystals used offer healing effects. They give a rejuvenating impact.

The concept behind crystal therapy is quite simple. In the part of the body affected by pain crystals and stones are applied to ease the pain.

These crystals work with the energy grids within their bodies. They are used to eliminate negative and positive energy. They also have an effect on the 10th, these result.

Experts offer crystal therapy. Although it's not a established whether it has a beneficial effect or it isn't.

However, the usage of this treatment demonstrates its advantages. This therapy has led to the health benefits. We can't conclusively say that this treatment does not provide some benefit.

Crystal therapy can be used to achieve complete relief from discomfort. The crystals and stones have been applied to various regions of the body been affected by pain. This therapy is extremely efficient in bringing relief.

Crystals and stones in the form they take when heated are placed in order to offer peace. The healing power hidden in stones assists to ease anxiety and stress. This creates an uplifting effect on the mind.

The most interesting aspect about crystal therapy is the way it does not have any adverse effects. It is used to alleviate tension and discomfort.

This is an extremely efficient method to reduce the pain but without any adverse effects. Natural stones and crystals can boost your health.

Chapter 12: Crystal Compendium

There are a myriad of crystals with distinctive characteristics. They have different energies and affect you in different ways as well as your daily life. These variations are due to the individual connection between you as well as your crystal. There are no two connections that are identical and it's up to you to develop your connection with your crystal and make use of crystals.

There is no scientific method for understanding the effects of crystals, and there are no standard for which crystals are best suited to what purpose. But, it is generally believed that certain crystals are more attuned to a particular reason or goal you've got to use it for. Below is a list of various crystals, listed according to alphabetical order. Each crystal is accompanied by a description of its purpose and the purpose it is most suitable for. The crystal guide is not meant designed to serve as a reference manual rather as a set of ideas on specific crystals and their specific applications.

If you're an avid follower to Astrology and Numerology the book contains information about the crystal that corresponds with which Zodiac sign, and what is the most is the most auspicious number.

Name of Crystal Aegirine

Description: A a dark green crystal with variations from black to brown. This is a tough, crystal of 6 with some streaks. It is found all over the globe , but is most prevalent in European countries like Greenland as well as Norway. It can also be found throughout Canada, the U.S. and Canada and in some regions of Russia.

The Elemental Connection: Fire and Earth

Zodiac Assemblies: Taurus

Number: 5

The background: Its name comes from Aegir the god of sea in the Norse mythology The crystal is associated with protection from elements.

The purpose The purpose of this crystal is to be one of the most powerful crystals believed to provide protection particularly against negative influences and energies. It guards against mental discord like anxieties, worries, and stress. It also protects against dependence and addiction.

Name of crystal: Agate

Description The crystal is part of the quartz group, and located within parts of the Southern Americas and some parts of Africa It has a hardness of 7.

The Elemental Connection: Earth

Zodiac Affinity: Gemini

Number: 7

Background: Named for the river that flows through Sicily This crystal is usually connected with prehistoric and early civilisations. It is intended to be utilized to provide stability.

Its purpose is to enhance the connection between your mind and body. It is a the source of your strength as it improves the body's capacity to keep pace with the determination and creativity that your brain has. Also, it is believed to be able to detect truth and falsehoods.

Name of crystal Amber

Description The crystal is one of the most distinctive crystals as it is made from Organic origins. It is made from the ashes of trees and other plants. It is very soft with a minimum two-inch hardness.

The Elemental Connection: Earth

Zodiac Affinity: Cancer

Number: 3

Background: Derived from electrical term, this stone releases the impression of an electric charge whenever it is touched. It is frequently utilized as a gemstone in jewelry and is often employed in huge quantities by the royals.

Main purpose: The primary function is purification. It is a powerful crystal that transforms old or negative energies into something beneficial and valuable. In addition to being a source for transformed positivity, this could also be used to create source of power.

Name of Crystal Amethyst

Description: A semi-precious crystal with a range in shades of violet. The finest quality of this crystal is found in Brazil. Its hardness is 7.

Elemental Affinity Wind

Zodiac Assemblies: Pisces

Number: 3

Background: It is associated in The Greek God of Wine, Dionysus This crystal protects against getting drunk and mental states of confusion that result from inability to control.

The purpose of this crystal is usually used during meditation because it helps to bring clarity to your mind. It is also believed to help you keep in touch to your intuition and help you awaken your psychic abilities that you might have.

The name of the crystal: Aquamarine

Description The sky blue crystal is a turquoise green crystal it is found in a variety of regions of Middle East and has a hardness of 7.

Elemental Affinity Water

Zodiac Affinity: Gemini

Number: 1

Background: Derived from Latin words which mean water, the word is used to symbolize the sea and the clarity it offers. This is the most traditional crystal that sailors use to shield them from harm when traveling.

The purpose: One of the most powerful crystals that can help to cleanse the mind and body from any excessive or violent energies. It also gives you the ability to release emotional baggage , or any other kind of burden you carry that could hinder your path through life.

Name of the Crystal Bloodstone

Description: Located in nearly every corner of the globe From Australia to US from Australia to India This crystal comes in various colors that can be found within one piece, ranging from bright yellow to deep purples, dark greens as well as reds.

Earth's Elemental Affinity Earth

Zodiac Affinity: Aries

Number: 6

Background: Named in honor of The Greek sun god the bloodstone was used in the past to talismans worn by soldiers going to battle. It can be used to heal physical injuries like wounds from war, and also as a source of strength.

Objective: Use the stone to increase your confidence and strength. Rely on the power of the bloodstone whenever you're faced with the toughest of challenges or when you need to make a crucial choice. It also helps help regulate hormonal changes, especially for women.

The name of the crystal: Quartz (Clear)

The description: One of the the most abundant minerals, all places around the globe is home to quartz. Its hardness is 7.

Elemental Affinity Water

Zodiac Affinity The Zodiac Affinity - All Signs

Number: 4

Background: From early times quartz has been used in rituals that are about looking into the future.

The purpose of quartz is that it is considered to be the go-to crystal that amplifies the effects of other crystals. Although it's powerful by itself to improve the clarity of mind and body but its main function is to help the crystals surrounding it to increase the power of the effect of the other crystal on it on you.

Name of Crystal Name of Crystal

Description It is one of the most popular crystals, and is favored because of its many colors. It's relatively soft, with a its hardness of just 4.

Elemental Affinity Wind

Zodiac Affinity: Capricorn

Number: 7

Background: If you're new to crystals Fluorite is a great choice due to the numerous colors available and its fairly affordable price.

The purpose Focus is the primary goal of this crystal. It is able to provide order, organization and structure. The crystal can provide you with stability and equilibrium. It is recommended to use it when you're at an era in your life that you're confused or not sure about what you should do.

Name of the Crystal Garnet

Description It is a deep maroon or almost brown-colored crystal, it is also found in different regions of the world. It is hardness of 7.

Earth's Elemental Affinity Earth

Zodiac Affinity: Aquarius

Number: 11

History: The crystal was also used by a wide range of people during the old times from royalty to lower soldiers, to guard against blood diseases and bad luck. It is also used by Eastern religions to symbolize of clarity.

Goal: It's designed to bring a calm feeling when facing something troubling or challenging. It is also designed to help you attain prosperity and wealth, as well as other things of the material world. It's also believed to make dreams come true.

Name of Crystal Jade

Description: Although it is usually considered to be part of the Eastern world Crystals like this can be located within Western countries. It comes in a variety of colors, from pure white to more common green. Its hardness is 6.

The Elemental Connection: Earth

Zodiac Assemblies: Taurus

Number: 5

The background: Crystals are generally connected to China and is even regarded as sacred and utilized to create the representations of gods.

The purpose: Fertility is the principal reason behind this crystal. It's also believed that it will aid owners in enhancing their happiness in life , and also assist people live their lives to the fullest.

Whatever thing in your existence not enough can be made more abundant with this crystal.

Crystal Name: Jasper

Description: With a majority of deep brown and red This crystal is distinguished by an interesting feature that is distinctive: spots on the surface. Its hardness is 7.

Earth's Elemental Affinity Earth

Zodiac Affinity: Virgo

Number: 6

Background: It is sold in various places, but is usually bought in India.

Its purpose is anything that is concerned with bodily functions, like breathing, digestion and circulation can be assisted through this mineral. It is naturally attuned to the healing abilities in the body. it is a great choice to help your body deal due to illness or other issues.

Name of the Crystal Lapis Lazuli

Description: It has an array of light blue to dark blue hues. It can be located throughout areas of Southern Americas and in some regions in the Middle East. Its hardness is 5.

Elemental Affinity Wind

Zodiac Affinity: Sagittarius

Number: 3

Background: Highly sought-after and coveted by Middle Eastern royalty, this crystal is utilized in many tools including knives, holy images to even makeup and , of course, jewelry.

The purpose of this crystal can be used to attain consciousness of oneself. If you're soul-searching or trying to connect with your own inner self through meditation, prayer or any kind of spiritual practice, this crystal should be used with these practices.

The Crystal's Name: Moonstone

Description typically white This crystal can be located throughout Burma, Australia and parts of Sri Lanka. Its hardness is 6.

Elemental Affinity Wind

Zodiac Affinity: Scorpio

Number: 4

Background: Named so because it is like the moon's hue when it shines. it's designed for use as a token of appreciation for newlyweds in order to inspire enthusiasm.

The purpose of this crystal is designed to tune the body and its hormones to the cycles of moon. This helps to prepare the body for maximum performance during romantic activities as well as other forms of exercise that require passion. It also improves the health because it is in connection with the creation of moments.

The crystal's name is Opal

Description: Because of the unique structure of its crystals Opal is able to emit different colors in addition to white. The majority of the supply of opal originates from Australia. Its hardness is 5.

Elemental Affinity Water

Zodiac Affinity: Libra

Number: 8

Background The different cultures have distinct reasons for this crystal. Some cultures use it to aid in healing, others for love and others use it as a lucky charm.

Main purpose: The primary function that the crystal serves is to serve as it is a source of confidence. It's intended to assist you in recognizing the potential of your skills and eliminate any doubt about making use of the crystals. It can also help get rid of any fears and boost your confidence.

Name of crystal Ruby

Description: Typically red in color and commonly found in Asian countries It has an abrasion of 9.

The Elemental Connection: Earth

Zodiac Affinity: Aries

Number: 3

Background: As one of the precious crystals of the four This crystal has been highly valued since prehistoric times due to the numerous positive characteristics it has including protection and energy, as well as passion.

The purpose of this crystal is to provide physical and sensual pleasure. are the primary goals for this stone. It's intended to bring happiness and connection to the material pleasures all over the globe. It's also designed to inspire you with energy and strength. It is also able to heal you from the effects of trauma, both physical and psychological.

Name of crystal: Topaz

Description It is found across Russia, Mexico, Japan and in other regions of the globe This crystal comes in a variety of colors , but it is typically yellow in hue. It is hard as 8.

Elemental Affinity Fire

Zodiac Affinity: Sagittarius

Number: 1

History: The crystal is believed to be initially used to boost the testosterone levels and increase the performance of males.

Its purpose: This crystal is designed to stimulate the mind and its faculties. It's all about increasing intelligence, knowledge and abilities. It's designed to boost imagination and mental health. When you face an issue that is complex, topaz will help bring clarity.

The name of the crystal: Diamond

Description: While it is commonly colored diamond, this gem is also colored from blue to yellow and can even be colored to uncommon pink diamond.

Elemental Affinity: All elements

Zodiac Assemblies: Taurus

Number: 7

Background It is the most durable known, having the toughness rating of 10. There are only a few regions around the globe that have this hardness, India and Africa being among them. It's a symbol of durability and permanence.

The purpose of this crystal is to be powerful detoxifier of negativity and negative energies that are present within the mind and body. It also helps boost your confidence as it represents the strength of your character. It also is believed to increase the brain and imagination.

Chapter 13: Using Crystals To Heal

There are a variety of methods to utilize crystals to heal. There are also a variety of crystals that are suitable for various problems, concerns and ailments. This book is not intended to inform anyone that you should utilize specific crystals for an end in mind, or else it isn't going to be effective. This book is not about that. is about. I'm here to guide you on your journey of deep learning journey to assist you in adapting the best ways that I have utilized crystals, and also the most efficient results for different issues.

Because there is numerous methods to utilize crystals to heal I've sketched a bit about all the common ways to utilize crystals for healing. This will help you learn the ropes and bolts before applying them to the appropriate crystals for each area of use. Be aware that you are able to utilize different crystals if those I have described don't resonate in your energy fields. The combination of crystals, techniques employed with them, and the way they are employed, is the elements that make a part of these healing methods most efficient.

Wearing or carrying your CRYSTAL

Being able to have crystals within your active fields is the most straightforward way to employ crystals. However does it necessarily mean it's the most effective? It's not always the case but a lot times there isn't. You have crystal energy within your energetic fields of vibration, but when you don't place it where you require it most, or keep it in place for a prolonged time period, it'll affect the signs of the disease, and it won't be the root cause. If you don't use this particular crystal until the problem is gone completely then it could return and the process starts all over again.

On the other hand the wearing or carrying of the crystal is beneficial if you would like to do or you want to be able to access these energy sources continuously. The most straightforward ways to achieve this is to simply carry stones in your pockets or purse, put the crystal as an ornamental packaging or other similar crystals strategies. This is fashionable and efficient!

When working with crystals in this line, be sure to get rid of them and wash them frequently, as they interact with your energetic fields, as well as the fields that you interact with. Therefore, ensure that you clean the crystals and set them up as often as is necessary!

Conclusion

Crystals can be utilized in many ways, ranging between jewelry Feng Shui and cleansing chakras. Each crystal comes with its own unique characteristics that aid in channeling the energy of earth. Each crystal has a distinct function, and by learning how to utilize these crystals to your advantage, you can change your life. It is a non-invasive way to boost your life! It isn't an original concept and has been used for quite a while. But, it's been becoming a popular alternative and holistic method of healing in the last few years. Learn how to heal yourself by using crystals is the most effective method to control your life.

Now that you're armed with the knowledge that you need on crystal healing, it's time to begin applying it to your daily life. Based on your requirements or the area of life that you'd like to focus on and use the right crystals. When it comes to healing with crystals it is essential to be patient and never give up on the power of their energy. You'll definitely see an improvement in your overall health however, it may require some time. In the meantime take the time to learn patience and remain consistent when working using crystals.